The Life and Times of
HENRY VII

ENDPAPERS Ptolemy and Amerigo Vespucci
from Martin Waldseemüller's map of
the world

OVERLEAF LEFT Henry VII as a young man:
portrait of the French school.
OVERLEAF RIGHT Richmond Castle in
Yorkshire, the centre of Henry Tudor's
earldom and honour. This illustration is taken
from an early fifteenth-century register of
the Honour of Richmond and shows the
castle surmounted by various coats of arms.
(Bodleian Ms Lyell 22f 21v)

The Life and Times of
HENRY VII

Neville Williams

Introduction by Antonia Fraser

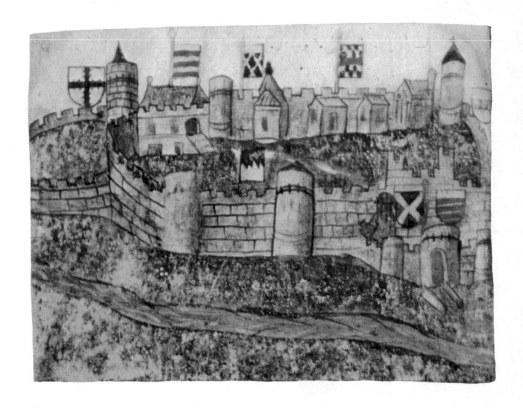

Book Club Associates, London

For my god-daughter, Sarah Green

© George Weidenfeld and Nicolson Limited
and Book Club Associates 1973

Series designed by Paul Watkins
Layout by Michael Fry
Filmset by Keyspools Limited, Golborne, Lancs
Printed in Great Britain by
C. Tinling & Co. Ltd, Prescot and London

Contents

Acknowledgments

Photographs and illustrations were supplied or are reproduced by kind permission of the following: The pictures on pages *14–15*, 32, *62*, *64*, 113 are reproduced by gracious permission of H.M. The Queen; on page 61 by courtesy of His Grace The Duke of Rutland; on page 201 by courtesy of the Earl of Yarborough; on page 213 by kind permission of the Dean and Chapter of Westminster; on page 63 by kind permission of the Dean and Canons of Windsor. Ashmolean Museum, Oxford: 107; National Bibliothek, Austria: 69, 147; Bibliothèque Arsenal: 125; Bibliothèque de la Ville, Sélestat: 103; Bodleian Library, Oxford: *3*, 58–9, 114/2; British Museum: 10–11, 16, 19, 22, 34–5, 38, 39, 55, 56–7, 122, 128–9, 131, 180–1, 187, *193*, 195, *208*; British Printing Corporation: *61*; Cambridge University Library: *95*; Trustees of the Chatsworth Settlement: 102; Master and Fellows of Corpus Christi, Cambridge: 46; Stanley Eost: 214–5; Mary Evans Picture Library: 117; John Fleming: 178, 179; Werner Forman: 41; John Freeman: 22, 27, 187; Giraudon: 20, 66, 125, 136, 152, 153, 198; Goldsmiths Librarian, University of London: 155; Harvard University Library: 71; Michael Holford Library: 130; Inner Temple; 178, 179; A. F. Kersting: 13, 42–3, 45, 96–7, 108, 140/1, 140/2, 166/1, 166/2; Kunsthistorisches Museum, Vienna: *64*, 75, 86, 87; Kupferstichkabinett, Berlin: 88; Edward Leigh: 118; Master and Fellows of Magdalen College, Oxford: *82–3*; Mansell Collection: 104–5, 146, 146–7, 148, 157; MAS: 200; Musée Calvet: *2*; National Library of Wales: 93; National Monuments Record (Crown Copyright) 50, 90, 207, 212/1, 212/2, 216; National Portrait Gallery: *52*, 111, *205*; Pegli Naval Museum: 149; La Pensée Universitaire: 203; Pepys' Library, Magdalene College, Cambridge: 118; Public Record Office (Crown Copyright): 106, 141, 159, 170, 185, 186, 210, 211; Royal College of Arms: 98–9; John Rylands Library: 114/1, 116; Scala: 68, 94; Master and Fellows of St John's College, Cambridge: *49*; Science Museum: 176/2, 177; Walter Scott: 44; Scottish National Portrait Gallery: 196/1; Society of Antiquaries: 29, 190; Staatsarchiv, Berlin: 160; Universiteits-Bibliothek, Amsterdam: endpapers; Victoria and Albert Museum: 27, 101, 163, 176/1, 196/2; Roger Viollet: 115

Numbers in italic indicate colour illustrations.

Picture research by Andra Nelki.

Introduction

'A SEMINAL MILESTONE' – so, with the benefit of hindsight, Neville Williams greets the memorable victory of Henry VII at Bosworth Field in 1485. The Middle Ages had fought their way to a finish: the Tudor monarchy was ushered in. In its own way the event was to be compared for importance with the coronation of Charlemagne in the history of Europe. Yet how little we know of the personality of the industrious, avaricious, pious Welshman – for that, essentially, was what Henry Tudor was – who now ascended the throne by right of conquest, if his actual hereditary claim was somewhat 'patchy'. In a reign of just under twenty-four years, he would now lay down the guidelines of Tudor despotism for his powerful royal descendants, the dazzling Henry VIII, the glorious Elizabeth. He would also leave his mark ineradicably on the institutions and organisation of England itself. Thus the study of the character and intentions of this remarkable if mysterious man becomes not only of interest in its own right, as Neville Williams amply proves, but also highly relevant to the course of English history.

In himself, Henry bridged the two eras in which he lived. A medieval childhood – he was the son of the famously learned Lady Margaret Beaufort – an emergence out of the Welsh mists enabling him to claim to be the conqueror of ancient prophecy who would restore the Welsh to the throne of the Britons – all this contrasted strangely with the later years of his reign. Now Henry showed little of the romance of his origins, but an excellent grasp of the new necessities of government, even if he was more of an energetic improviser than a deliberate innovator. A Spanish observer wrote that the King's love of money was so great that he cheerfully spent all his time 'in writing the accounts of his expenses in his own hand'. That might be so, but it was a valuable ruler indeed who was able to leave his country solvent at his death. In the same way, Henry VII registered another achievement which would have seemed exceptional to his ancestors: he died in his bed in 1509, master in his own house, having virtually put an end to the private armies and wars of the nobility which had bedevilled England in past centuries. Henry VII had begun the moulding of a nation. 'Vivat, vivat' the crowd called to the King as he passed, and he had surely deserved the acclaim.

Neville Williams, with all the expertise at his command, does not rest his picture on Henry's character alone. Here is also the heraldic pageant of late fifteenth century England unfolded, for pageant was how it was and how the monarch intended it to be, with his sumptuous royal palaces, his display at Court, aimed not at personal ostentation (he was privately frugal) but at the public demonstration of kingly power. Here too are the many and varied individuals of the age, when the 'New Learning' and also the new religious thinking began to be spread abroad: Erasmus, Colet, Fisher, the explorer Cabot, Caxton, the historian Polydore Vergil, the poet Skelton. Henry VII's is the central portrait of a rich historical gallery.

Antonia Fraser

Preface

IN THIS SHORT BIOGRAPHY, I have emphasised that the man who founded the Tudor dynasty, in an epoch when Europe was in ferment, was essentially medieval in outlook. At one time historians, taking much of the propaganda of the Tudor age at its face value, were tempted into elevating Henry VII into a new-style monarch whose accession was a watershed. Henry's achievement, it is now clear, lay less in original developments in the art of government than in reconciling his subjects to his rule and in making England a force in European politics. His role was much more that of the last of the medieval kings than that of the first 'modern' monarch in England.

I am particularly indebted to Margaret Willes for her generous advice on so many points during the book's preparation and owe much to Andra Nelki, who selected the illustrations. I also wish to thank Annabel Clover for her skilful typing of my manuscript.

N.W.

1
Lancastrian
Heritage
1457-85

THE BATTLE OF BOSWORTH FIELD, fought on 22 August 1485, seemed to many Englishmen – despite Richard III's death in action – no more than another engagement in the episodic campaigns between Yorkist and Lancastrian factions that had plagued England since the end of the Hundred Years' War and had seen the crown change hands five times. The victory regarded by posterity as decisive could so easily have been reversed. According to the realistic dictum that 'he who lost the day lost the kingdom also', Henry Tudor's immediate hold on his realm was insecure. He remained haunted by the thought that another army as small as his own could overturn his triumph, and it was not until his later years that he ceased to feel in danger. It was only with the benefit of hindsight, with the new dynasty successfully established, that the year 1485 has become regarded as a seminal date in England's story – a veritable milestone like Charlemagne's coronation in 800, or the French Revolution of 1789. The paradox of the reign was that in a changing world, with horizons expanding in so many directions, Henry was still in outlook a medieval King, and yet he was so successful in his dynastic ambitions that the crown of England has remained ever since in the line of his heirs.

Henry Tudor was born at Pembroke Castle on 28 January 1457, the only son of Edmund Tudor, Earl of Richmond, and the Lady Margaret Beaufort. He was not born into the purple in a royal palace, his arrival in the world was not heralded by national rejoicing, nor was he a child aware from a tender age that he was different in kind and degree from other boys because he was destined for a crown. The circumstances of his birth were unpropitious, for he was very much the child of civil war. His mother, still under fourteen years old, had been a widow for twelve weeks, for Edmund Tudor, sent to take control of South Wales, had been captured by Yorkists the previous summer and imprisoned in Carmarthen Castle, where he died in November, aged about twenty-six. In her adversity, the Lady Margaret was comforted by her strong religious convictions, to which she held firmly throughout her life, and was protected by her brother-in-law, Jasper Tudor, Earl of Pembroke, who brought her to his castle. When John Leland visited Pembroke towards the end of Henry VIII's reign he noted 'the castle

PREVIOUS PAGES John Talbot, Earl of Shrewsbury, (1413–60) presenting a book to Henry VI and Margaret of Anjou, while the Court looks on.

12

standeth hard by the wall on a hard rock and is very large and
strong, being double-warded. In the outer ward I saw the
chamber where Henry VII was born, in knowledge whereof a
chimney is now made, with the arms and badges of the King.'
A few years before this visit, Edmund Tudor's remains had
been removed by royal command of his grandson from the
Greyfriars in Carmarthen to a place of honour in St David's
Cathedral.

Henry's paternal grandfather, Owen Tudor of Anglesey
stock, had entered the household of Henry V as a page, until
service at Agincourt earned him early promotion to the ranks
of the Squires of the Body to the King. Welsh medieval
genealogy is fraught with pitfalls, but in the case of the Tudor
family the lineage is unusually difficult to disentangle. Henry
VII, proud of his Welsh ancestry, had prepared, by a herald, an
abbot and a Welsh-speaking canon, a pedigree which enthusias-
tically linked him not only with such princes as Cadwallader
the Great (who died in 1172) but even with such mythical
figures as 'Trojan Brutus', a putative ruler of Dark Age
Britain. The most that can be said with certainty is that an
ancestor, Ednyfed Vaughan, was a competent administrator in
the service of Llewelyn the Great in the early thirteenth century.

After Henry V's death Owen Tudor stayed on at Court; the

Pembroke Castle: the
birthplace of Henry VII.
The great round keep and
inner bailey date from
c. 1200, while the curtain
walls were added in the
mid-thirteenth century.
The castle was held by
Jasper Tudor in the 1450s,
and Henry was probably
born in one of the towers
of the curtain walls.
After Jasper's flight in
1461 the earldom and
castle of Pembroke passed
to William Herbert, who
brought up Henry Tudor
in his household.

13

The family of Henry VII with St George and the Dragon. In the background stand two fantastic buildings, with St George slaying the dragon to protect Princess Cleodolinde. In the foreground, below canopies decorated with the badges of the Tudors, kneel Henry VII and his Queen, Elizabeth of York, with their seven children. This painting in its original version is thought to have been an altarpiece at the royal palace of Sheen, and could well have been painted for a tournament held there in 1492 when Garter arms were granted to various knights, hence the allusion to St George.

15

young Queen-Dowager, Catherine of Valois, appointed him Clerk of her Wardrobe, and they soon fell in love. The secret of their marriage (probably in 1425) was so well kept that it was perhaps not until the birth of their fifth child, at Hatfield, that the King's Council, frightened of the political effects of scandal, forced them to separate. Queen Catherine retired to Bermondsey Abbey, where she died the following year, while her young sons were initially placed in the care of the Abbess of Barking. Owen took sanctuary at Westminster, but surrendered on promise of a safe-conduct to Wales. However, on the orders of the Regent, Humphrey of Gloucester, he was arrested and put in Newgate gaol but succeeded in escaping to the Principality. Once Henry VI came of age, his half-brothers, Edmund and Jasper Tudor, and their father Owen, were assured of royal protection and favour. (Altogether Owen Tudor had three sons and two daughters by Catherine de Valois – Edmund and Jasper, noted here, Owen and Catherine, who both entered religious orders, and Jacira, who married Reynold, Lord Grey of Wilton.) With the outbreak of civil war they showed themselves faithful Lancastrians. Owen was taken prisoner at Mortimer's Cross in 1461 and on Edward IV's orders was beheaded in Hereford market-place, saying as he went before his executioner, 'that head shall lie on the stock that was wont to lie on Queen Catherine's lap'. A mad woman combed the hair and washed the face of the severed head, set on the market cross. Owen's son Jasper escaped from the battlefield to rejoin Queen Margaret of Anjou.

Edmund Tudor, the eldest of Owen's three sons, had been created Earl of Richmond in 1452 and formally declared legitimate by Parliament. The next year Jasper was created Earl of Pembroke. He was to play a leading part in Henry's life before the overthrow of Richard III. War and exile had left him a bachelor until, in his mid-fifties, he married a widow; his only child was an illegitimate daughter, Helen, who became the mother of Stephen Gardiner, Bishop of Winchester, destined to preach Henry VIII's funeral oration. The third brother, Owen like his father, outlived his generation by steering clear of politics, for he had become a monk at Westminster Abbey and when he died in 1502 Henry VII paid for his funeral.

Henry's mother was one of the most remarkable women of

OPPOSITE The ancestry of Henry VI: on the left are ranged his Valois predecessors, and on the right his Plantagenet ancestors. The figures at the foot of the page are, on the left, Richard, Duke of York, Regent of England and the father of Edward IV and Richard III, and on the right, Humphrey, Duke of Gloucester, Regent and Henry VI's uncle.

the century – a blue-stocking, devout yet thrice married (not counting her months as a child bride to Suffolk's son). She was ambitious for her only child, from whom she was parted for all but a few of his first twenty-eight years, yet Lady Margaret remained incredibly discreet in these difficult times, almost to the point of disinterestedness. She had a flair for fading into the background, turning her everyday life into a holy retreat. She was of almost royal lineage. Her great-grandfather was John of Gaunt who, after his second wife's death, had made an honest woman of his mistress, Catherine Swynford, sister-in-law to the poet Chaucer. Their brood of children were named Beauforts after the Beaufort Castle in France in which at least one of them had been born. Though born on the wrong side of the blanket, they had been legitimised by Parliament. The eldest son, John, was created Earl of Somerset by Richard II, and his brother Henry became a Cardinal. Somerset's second son, another John Beaufort who had succeeded as the third earl on his eldest brother's premature death in 1418, died in 1444 leaving a daughter, Margaret, aged three. When she was nine years old she was brought to Court during the heyday of her guardian, William de la Pole, Duke of Suffolk, the effective ruler of the realm, who affianced her to his son. Later, when the Duke fell from power, men accused him of aiming at bringing the boy nearer the throne through this alliance – even though King Henry IV had decreed that none of his Beaufort cousins could succeed. But Suffolk had found a wealthier heiress for his son and Henry VI was anxious to arrange a marriage between Margaret and his half-brother, Edmund Tudor. Tradition has it that the girl was much confused about her future spouse but that as a result of a vision she became convinced she should wed Richmond. Their marriage, as we have seen, was tragically brief; at thirteen she was a widow, great with child and pinning her hopes on a son.

After her son's triumphs, Margaret wrote to him on his birthday, ending her letter in 1501 'this day of St Agnes, that I did bring into this world my good and gracious prince, king and only-beloved son', with her memories of Pembroke Castle and the tribulations which followed. By then a great lady, far above the political fray, she was more than satisfied with Henry's discharge of his duties. To the end he respected her,

John Beaufort, 1st Earl of Somerset, Margaret Beaufort's grandfather and son of John of Gaunt by Catherine Swynford. He is depicted kneeling before a scene of the Annunciation, from the early fifteenth-century *Beaufort Book of Hours*.

not merely as his mother or as a most cultivated and devout lady, but as the heiress of the House of Lancaster, through whom his imperfect title to the throne of England derived.

After Edward IV seized the crown in 1461, Pembroke Castle, where Margaret and her child had been living with Jasper Tudor, fell to the Yorkists and they were placed under the guardianship of William Herbert. Since Herbert was also granted Pembroke Castle and Jasper's earldom of Pembroke, the boy did not need to change his residence. Though separated from his mother, who by now had married the Lancastrian Sir Henry Stafford, the boy found in Herbert an admirable substitute for his father. His schooling was taken seriously and he was brought up as a prospective husband for Herbert's daughter Maud. When he was twelve, however, Henry's world collapsed around him, for the Earl of Warwick, Richard Neville the Mighty, had his guardian executed for alleged treachery. Perhaps during this crisis Lady Margaret managed to have her son with her. At any rate when Warwick became a Kingmaker the next year, restoring Henry VI to the throne, Jasper Tudor was able to return from exile and brought his nephew to Court;

19

it was probably Henry's first visit to England. Jasper hoped that the boy's earldom of Richmond might be restored to him, but it proved impolitic to have it taken away from Edward IV's younger brother, the Duke of Clarence. Henry VI, seeing his young nephew from Wales for the first time, greeted him, it is said, with the prophetic words, 'this truly, this is he unto whom both we and our adversaries must yield and give over the dominion'. It was as if the King realised that within a year his own line would be extinct, and that young Henry would become the true heir of Lancaster.

We know little of Henry's early years, as he moved among the castles in the Principality and changed guardians with the

Edward IV in battle: from a version of the Chronicles of Philip de Commines produced in the early sixteenth century.

fortunes of civil war. For a Welshman he was tall, and though his hair was dark, he boasted a fair complexion. We know that he was athletic and rode well. These early years of tribulation certainly nurtured an instinct for survival. Henry had an inner toughness and was determined to make his way in a hostile world, although the dice seemed loaded against him, and in exile this trait in his character hardened. From his youth he remained a devoted son of the Church, yet he was too active and vigorous to be withdrawn from the world and too independent to let himself be dominated by priests and confessors.

The Lancastrian restoration was short-lived, for Edward IV recovered the crown in the fog at Barnet on Easter Day 1471, when the Kingmaker was slain. Soon afterwards, the Lancastrians, with a fresh army from Wales and the western shires, put up a brave fight for Queen Margaret of Anjou at Tewkesbury, but the Yorkists again triumphed. It was no longer safe for Henry of Richmond to stay quietly in Wales, and so to avoid capture by the Yorkists Jasper Tudor made for the coast with his nephew and a few hand-picked companions. They were nearly captured at Chepstow; at Pembroke, their home town, they were recognised by enemies and locked up for a week; but they managed to escape to reach Tenby where they took a boat for France. A gale forced them to land in Brittany, still an independent duchy, where they were welcomed by Duke Francis II and given political asylum. For the moment Henry's adventures were over.

The year 1471 was a disastrous one for the Lady Margaret, for apart from her son's narrow escape into exile, she lost her husband, Sir Henry Stafford. Two years later she married again; her third husband was Thomas, Lord Stanley, a trusted servant of Edward IV. Sensibly she accepted the Yorkist regime, but contrived to keep up a correspondence with her son in Brittany and was already planning for him to marry one of King Edward's daughters.

Edward IV continued to press the Duke of Brittany to surrender his guests, for with the deaths of both Henry VI and his son Prince Edward in 1471, Richmond had become the head of the House of Lancaster, and as such was a potential threat to Edward's throne. After five years King Edward became more persuasive, assuring Duke Francis that his intentions were most

Henry Tudor as a young man: from the *Recueil d'Arras*.

sincere, since he wanted Henry Tudor home to marry one of his daughters. By now Edward had a secure hold on his realm and could afford to be magnanimous, while the presence of Richmond's mother at Court, as wife of the Lord Steward, would have been some guarantee for Henry's safety. But Henry was convinced that not even his mother's influence could save him from certain murder once he reached England. In 1476 Duke Francis agreed to hand him over to an English embassy, yet connived at his escape; for when the envoys took Henry to St Malo for a passage home, he feigned a fever and was removed to sanctuary. Edward IV accepted the inevitable and

22

paid the Duke to keep Richmond in Brittany, so there he remained throughout his impressionable years.

His fourteen years' sojourn at the Court of Brittany – a duchy rich in Celtic associations – taught Henry the powerful hold on people's imagination of the old romances associated with the legendary Arthur. His knowledge of French was a good deal better than his command of English, and what he read of the Breton versions of the Arthurian cycle fitted in with what he had been told of the fiery prognostications of the Welsh bards. Shrewdly he vowed to name his first-born legitimate son Arthur.

There was one legacy of the years of exile, for Henry became enamoured of a Breton girl who bore him a son, named Roland de Velville. Eventually the lad came to England and was knighted by his father on the field of battle at Blackheath in 1497. Roland was soon afterwards appointed Constable of Beaumaris Castle, where he lived until his death in 1527; thus a Tudor returned to Anglesey, from which the family had sprung. There was never a hint that Roland, like Charles II's Monmouth, might prove a political embarrassment. He married a Welsh girl and their granddaughter, Catherine of Berain, proudly acknowledged her cousinage to Elizabeth I.

The revulsion of so many of the Yorkist nobility at Richard III's usurpation of the throne in June 1483 made them weigh carefully the rival claims of the young Earl of Richmond. Rumours of the murder of the Princes in the Tower had, indeed, brought Henry nearer to the throne. Moreover, in April 1484, two months after Richard's son Edward had been declared heir apparent, the eleven-year-old boy died at Middleham, removing yet another obstacle. At first Richard contemplated naming as his heir Edward, Earl of Warwick, his brother Clarence's son, but in the end he preferred another nephew, John de la Pole, Earl of Lincoln, who was now granted the reversion of the estates of Lady Margaret Beaufort. For the present all was playing into Henry Tudor's hands; although once he became King he was to be plagued by Warwick and his impersonators and by Lincoln, while the adherents of 'the White Rose of England' would continue to intrigue long into his son's reign.

Detail from the Rous Roll, which was produced by John Rous, a chantry priest of Guy's Cliff near Warwick, to show the Earls of Warwick and their families. This part shows Richard III with his Queen, Anne Neville – the daughter of Warwick the Kingmaker – and their only son, Edward, Prince of Wales, who died in 1484.

A mere fifteen weeks after Richard's coronation, Buckingham's rebellion broke out in favour of Richmond. Henry Stafford, second Duke of Buckingham and nephew by marriage to Lady Margaret, had been Richard's chief ally in securing the crown. Sickened by his master's tyrannical behaviour, he pondered his own claim to the throne, as a descendant of Thomas of Woodstock, Duke of Gloucester, the youngest son of Edward III. However he was finally persuaded by John Morton, Bishop of Ely, who was in his custody at Brecon Castle, to lead a rising in the name of Henry Tudor. He asserted that Henry should undertake to marry his niece Elizabeth of York. In September 1483 Buckingham wrote inviting him to land in England to deliver the realm from tyranny. One can imagine Henry Tudor's thrill at reading this invitation, signed not by a disaffected Lancastrian, but by a man until now the mainstay of Yorkist rule, whose marriage had allied him with the Woodvilles. Bishop Morton used as an agent Christopher Urswick, Lady Margaret's confessor, who carried messages to her and to the Queen-Dowager, Elizabeth Woodville, who remained in sanctuary with her daughters at Westminster Abbey. There were to be simultaneous risings in Wales, the West Country and the Home Counties at St Lukestide so that Henry could be greeted as a deliverer when he landed. Elizabeth Woodville's son, the Marquess of Dorset and the Courtenays vouched for Devonshire, Sir Richard Woodville and his brother, the Bishop of Salisbury, for the men of Wiltshire, Sir John Fogge for Kent and Sir William Norris for Berkshire. Except in wild Wales it was hatred of Richard III rather than enthusiasm for Henry that motivated the rebels.

But that autumn luck was all against the disaffected, for the men of Kent rose prematurely, giving Richard time to make plans. Buckingham's defection so angered him that he castigated the Duke as 'the most untrue creature living ... there never was falser traitor purveyed for'. Buckingham planned to take his army across the Severn to join forces with the men of Devon raised by the Bishop of Exeter and Sir Edward Courtenay, yet heavy rains had so swollen the river that it was impassable; the Duke retreated to Shropshire, where he was to be betrayed, and went to his execution at Salisbury before the King on 2 November. Richard had marched swiftly to the West to find that the leaders had mostly fled, and that opposition to him was lukewarm. At Exeter he executed Sir Thomas St Leger, who had married his own sister Anne. Storms in the Channel had delayed Henry's arrival at Poole until his cause was lost, so he sailed on west. At Plymouth he was invited ashore by men claiming that they were adherents of Buckingham, but Henry knew this was a trap, and he left the Sound for Brittany, hoping for better success in the future. In preparation for this later attempt, he took a solemn oath in Rennes Cathedral on Christmas Day 1483 that once he was King of England he would marry Princess Elizabeth, heiress of the House of York.

Besides sounder strategy, Henry's cause needed greater enthusiasm. At this time his greatest asset was his Welsh blood.

Two decisive battles had been fought during the wars in the Marches of Wales – Mortimer's Cross and Tewkesbury – both defeats for the Lancastrian cause, but if Henry mustered a strong following from the Principality, England could be invaded and the Yorkist regime overturned. The men from the far west, who still regarded Jasper Tudor as the rightful Earl of Pembroke, and the chieftains from the north, would unite in what was for them essentially a Welsh cause, not a Lancastrian one. In this great era of Celtic poetry the bards – seers as much as poets – rallied men to Henry Tudor's support. David Llwyd ap Llywelyn from Machynlleth, perhaps the most forceful voice among them, foretold that the Prince, like Arthur of old, would come to rescue the Welsh people from Saxon thraldom. Henry Tudor was to be another Owen Glendower, a long-awaited Messiah. It is in the bardic prophecies that Henry is described as the descendant of Cadwallader and Brutus – poetic licence that the royal genealogists were to extend. Thus was Henry's cause proclaimed with a religious fervour in the mountains and valleys. When Henry pledged himself to marry Elizabeth of York, the Welsh remembered the Princess's own Celtic descent, through the Mortimers, from a daughter of Llewelyn the Great himself.

Though initially a disaster, the failure of Buckingham's rebellion had one great effect on Henry's fortunes, for the conspirators who escaped from England came to swell his little Court, first in Brittany, then in France. Others who saw Richard III as a fiendish usurper and were convinced of his responsibility for the murder of Edward V and his brother, looked to Henry of Richmond as the man of the future, the leader of an opposition to the Yorkist regime who presented himself as an effective alternative ruler of England, despite his weak hereditary claim. To Brittany came Edward Courtenay, John, Lord Wells, who was to marry Edward IV's daughter Cecily, and Edward Woodville. They were joined by men of the calibre of Edward Poynings, Richard Guildford and Giles Daubeney, all experienced soldiers who would prove themselves competent administrators. Richard Fox threw up his study of canon law at Paris University to serve the future King, while Bishop Morton of Ely (who after the collapse of his protégé's rebellion had escaped via the Fens in disguise to Flanders)

MISERICORDIA

Christopher Urswick, Lady Margaret Beaufort's confessor, who acted as agent for Bishop Morton to send messages to Lady Margaret and to Elizabeth Woodville, the Queen-Dowager, during the reign of Richard III. His memorial brass lies in Hackney Church, though he ended his days as Dean of Windsor.

at length came to kiss Henry's hand. A notable recruit to the Lancastrian cause was John de Vere, 13th Earl of Oxford, who had led an adventurous life since the Battle of Barnet. He had tried to land in Essex in 1473 to lead a rising against Edward IV and had then seized St Michael's Mount in Cornwall. Captured on the fall of the fort, he was imprisoned in Hammes Castle near Calais. In 1485, however, Oxford persuaded the captain of Hammes, James Blunt, not only to connive at his escape but to join him in rallying to Henry Tudor at Angers. Oxford, now forty-three, was easily the most distinguished of Henry's supporters, for he had a reputation as a noted tactician.

Richard was now adamant that Duke Francis should surrender Henry, and sugared his threats with bribes. The aged Duke, who had supported the émigré for more than a dozen years and more recently had borne the heavier burden of entertaining his growing entourage at his board, was now mentally deranged and his Treasurer, Pierre Landois, was quite prepared to sell Henry to the English. This scheme became known to the faithful Morton, who sent Christopher Urswick to warn Richmond in the nick of time. Henry arranged for his uncle and a few chosen men to make their way to the French frontier, and having despatched Urswick to France to arrange his asylum with King Charles VIII, he soon joined them by an indirect route, changing clothes with a servant in a forest and fleeing over the border into Anjou no more than an hour before a posse of Landois's horsemen reached the frontier. Soon afterwards, the Duke of Brittany recovered sufficiently to help Henry's main body of supporters join him at Langleais and then at Paris. Preparations were in train to embark at Harfleur.

In England, Richard III at last succeeded in inducing Elizabeth Woodville, the Queen-Dowager, to leave sanctuary at Westminster with her five daughters. He gave the most solemn assurances for their safety, as though there was still a chance of men believing he was innocent of the deaths of Edward V and his brother of York, who had 'ceased to appear altogether' in the gardens of the Tower where they formerly had been seen playing. There is no more forceful indictment of Richard's character than the fact that the King was forced to deny publicly before the Mayor and aldermen of London current rumours that he had poisoned his wife. After Queen Anne

OPPOSITE The Tudor image of Richard III. In strong contrast to the portrait of Richard in the Queen's Collection, which was probably based on a study from life, this is a hostile view of the King, produced in the sixteenth century, following the character study drawn by Sir Thomas More. Thus he is depicted with a broken sword, and with one shoulder perceptibly higher than the other.

Neville's death in 1485, Richard had designs on his niece Elizabeth of York, to trump Henry Tudor's bid for her hand, yet he found a marriage with her out of the question politically and sent her off to his castle at Sheriff Hutton in Yorkshire. Those were the days when Richard and his chief henchmen, Catesby, Ratcliffe and Lovell, were lampooned in the rhyme:

> The Cat, the Rat, and Lovell our Dog
> Rulen all England under a Hog

– the boar being Richard's emblem, which would soon face Richmond's red dragon.

Henry stiffened his supporters in Wales and elsewhere by sending letters proclaiming his 'rightful claim, due and lineal inheritance' to the crown, which would be won after depriving 'that homicide and unnatural tyrant, which now unjustly bears dominion over you'. One such letter, 'given under our signet', was sent to Rhys ap Thomas in South Wales where Henry planned to land. Richard, sensing that invasion was imminent, issued his proclamation warning all true Englishmen to be ready to repel the pretender, since Henry's claim to rule in his stead was baseless as he was 'descended of bastard blood both of the father's side and of his mother's side'. A chronicler was to describe Richard's disdain for his opponent by using the pithy phrase – 'an unknown Welshman, whose father I never knew, nor him personally saw'.

It could not be disputed that Henry was indeed relatively unknown in England, which he had visited but once, and had not been in his native Wales for half his life. Despite Richard's unpopularity, no one could predict how Englishmen, in contrast to the Welsh, would react to Henry's invasion. Yorkshire would assuredly stand loyal to Richard, yet much depended on whether the Stanleys in Lancashire and the north-west and Henry Percy, the Earl of Northumberland, in the north would fight for him. Before quitting Harfleur on 1 August, Henry left with Charles VIII, as hostages for the French loan of 60,000 francs advanced to him, two former Yorkists, the Marquess of Dorset and Lord Bourchier, whose loyalty he suspected. His force cannot have exceeded three thousand men, over half of them French mercenaries – that is to say convicts who had acquired their freedom on undertaking military service.

30

Unlike the attempt in the autumn of 1483, this enterprise was blessed with fine weather and, thanks to the 'soft southern wind', Henry Tudor's flotilla sailed into Milford Haven on the west coast of Pembrokeshire on 8 August to anchor in Dale road, a secluded stretch of water to the north side of Milford. On going ashore, Henry kissed the soil of Wales and recited in Latin the Psalmist's verse 'Be thou my judge, O Lord, for I have walked innocently.' He dubbed sixteen of his followers knights, including Edward Courtenay, Edward Poynings and John Fortescu, who was serving his term as Sheriff of Essex. Soon after disembarkation they were joined by Rhys ap Thomas and other leading men of Pembrokeshire, anxious to renew their friendship with Jasper Tudor, their own Earl, and to swear fealty to his nephew. The next day they reached Haverford West and began their difficult trek through the Prescelly Mountains and on to Cardigan. Fears that Sir Walter Herbert was to intercept them with a large force proved groundless. It had been decided that Henry should keep his army to the coast road, while the force being mustered by Rhys ap Thomas would take the inland route, partly to prevent bickering between French and Welsh, partly to conceal the invaders' presence for as long as possible. *En route* both armies gained recruits. It was not until Henry reached Machynlleth, where he crossed the River Dove, and was joined near the Long Mountain by the South Wales army captained by Rhys and also by men from the north of the Principality under their chieftains, that news reached Richard III at Nottingham that they had landed. By 15 August Shrewsbury was welcoming the invader – the same men who had surrendered the Duke of Buckingham two years earlier. On they went, to Stafford, Lichfield and Tamworth and along Watling Street; they had reached the heart of England unopposed, and were now within striking distance of Richard's army.

The battle was fought south-west of Market Bosworth. Richard's army outnumbered Henry's – perhaps ten thousand men to six thousand – but significantly only nine peers had obeyed the King's summons to the field of battle. With no experience of war, Henry prudently stayed in the rear, and whatever wish he may have had to be in the thick of the fighting, his person was too valuable for exposure to needless

THE DUKE OF KILLED AT NORFOLKE BOSWORTH FEILD

Jockey of norfolk
For Dickon thy

be not too bold
master is bought
and sold

danger. Thus Oxford commanded the vanguard. Richard had entered the campaign in good spirits and although deserted by the Earl of Northumberland – who kept his troops as bystanders to the battle, effectively blocking the King's line of retreat – betrayed by the Stanleys and bereft of his main commander, John Howard, Duke of Norfolk – who fell early in the action – his courage did not fail him. He rode down Ambien Hill with his household knights-at-arms to charge straight at Henry's bodyguard and challenge him to a personal fight. The King killed Henry's standard-bearer, but was soon surrounded by Sir William Stanley's horsemen. He was toppled from his great horse to be battered to death, shouting at the end 'Treason! Treason! Treason!' His corpse was stripped and taken on a horse to Leicester to show the incredulous that Henry was master of the kingdom.

Ratcliffe, Ferrers the Constable of the Tower, and Robert Brackenbury, were among the Yorkist dead; Norfolk's eldest son Surrey and Catesby among the prisoners, the latter being executed two days later. Lovell 'our Dog' and Humphrey Stafford had fled from the field, determined to fight another day. Northumberland, who had stayed neutral in the battle, remained at the neighbouring village of Sutton Cheney ready to pay homage to the new King when summoned. The tale of the crown of England that Richard had worn over his helmet being found under a thorn bush is apochryphal, yet the words which Shakespeare put into Henry's mouth, with victory assured after a bloody fight, somehow ring true: 'England hath long been mad and scarred herself.' He would bring a return to sanity and heal the old wounds.

OPPOSITE John Howard, 1st Duke of Norfolk, Richard III's principal commander at Bosworth. Before the battle, a note was found warning Howard: 'Jockey of Norfolk be not too bold, for Dickon thy master is bought and sold', and this is inserted on the portrait. John Howard fell early in the battle and this considerably demoralised Richard's troops.

2 The Founding of the

Dynasty 1485-7

E XILE HAD GIVEN Henry Tudor an instinct for survival – no more than Charles Stuart did he want to go on his travels again once he had come into his own. He was not by nature an adventurer and would, as far as possible, aim at overcoming his enemies by statecraft, so that against all the odds, as it seemed in 1485, he was to die in his bed in the twenty-fourth year of his reign. Near penury during his years in Brittany as a begging guest made him value money for what it could buy; accordingly as King he took the keenest interest in financial problems so that his carefulness became a byword. Henry took pleasure in auditing accounts himself and was only the second English sovereign in two centuries to bequeath to his successor a credit balance.

Before Richard III's corpse had reached Leicester, Henry's trusted servant Sir Robert Willoughby was on his way to Sheriff Hutton Castle in Yorkshire to take custody of Edward Plantagenet, the ten-year-old Earl of Warwick, who was to be despatched to the Tower of London as the chief competitor for the throne. He was also to make arrangements for Princess Elizabeth of York, also in the castle, to be brought with due honour to Westminster. Henry could not feel secure until the other principal claimant to his crown, John de la Pole, Earl of Lincoln, who had fled from the field of battle, was also in his hands. Pledged to marry Elizabeth, whom he had never seen, Henry was adamant that their marriage must be postponed until after his own coronation; though the Princess, as heiress of the House of York, was far too important to be allowed to marry another man, English or foreign, he must not make it appear that he owed his throne to her.

His weak personal claim to the throne paled before the outcome of Bosworth Field. Henry had accepted the invitation of Richard's rebellious subjects to put his claim to the test of trial by battle in which he had defeated and slain the reigning King. Indisputably he was *de facto* monarch and as such there was little doubt on the score of being the legitimate ruler by descent. To consolidate his position as effective ruler of England, Henry issued writs for Parliament to meet on 7 November, but eight days before it assembled he was crowned with great ceremony in Westminster Abbey. Old Archbishop Bourchier was too feeble to perform more than the anointing and crowning, so most of the elaborate ritual was ordered by the two Lancastrian stalwarts Bishops Morton of Ely and Courtenay of Exeter. In the secular ceremonial the peers closest to Henry, his uncle Jasper, his step-father Lord Stanley, by now Earl of Derby, and the Earl of Oxford were prominent. In the banquet in Westminster Hall, Sir Robert Dymock, the King's Champion, who not thirty months past had performed the same office for Richard III, rode into the Hall with his courser decked out in rich trappings of the Cadwallader arms to issue his customary challenge. Henry would have challengers enough in the years ahead, but none present disputed his sovereign power and the day for which he had been preparing for a dozen years passed without incident. The plague which had troubled London in high summer had vanished, and though the scaffolding of a stand erected for sightseers at Westminster collapsed, no one was hurt, which was taken as a good augury.

When Parliament opened, Henry was greeted as a second Joshua, divinely sent to rescue his people, and the Commons petitioned that, to remove all doubts, an Act should be passed declaring the inheritance of the crown to have come as of right to Henry and the heirs of his body, and this evoked the assent of the Lords. Acts of attainder were passed against the enemies defeated at Bosworth and the King was granted the revenue of the customs for life. Just before rising for Christmas both Houses urged Henry to honour his promise to marry Elizabeth of York, 'from which by the grace of God many hoped there would arise offspring of the race of Kings for the comfort of the whole realm'. For this the Pope's dispensation was necessary, as they were sufficiently related, being fourth cousins twice removed, although they anticipated the arrival of the final document from Rome. The wording of this papal bull of Innocent VIII, licensing their marriage, reinforced Henry's position, as it threatened with excommunication anyone who challenged his kingship and he had this fulsome recognition by the head of the Church printed as a broadsheet and sent throughout the realm.

The royal marriage was performed on 18 January 1486 at Westminster, but before then Henry and Elizabeth had in fact been living together. A consort's coronation was promised her once she had delivered the heir she was already carrying.

Elizabeth was nearly twenty-one, eight years younger than her husband, and a considerable beauty, for she was tall for a woman, of fair complexion with golden tresses, and her effigy in Westminster Abbey bears witness to her graceful features. Though not a scholar of the calibre of her mother-in-law, of whom she lived in some awe, Elizabeth had been well-schooled in Latin, French and Spanish. She was to bear Henry seven children, of whom three survived her: Margaret, the future Queen of James IV of Scotland, born in 1489; Henry, destined to succeed his father as King, born in June 1491; and Mary, born March 1495, who was briefly the last wife of Louis XII of

LEFT AND RIGHT Two details from the Rous Roll showing Edward, Earl of Warwick, and his sister Margaret, who later married Reginald Pole and became Countess of Salisbury. Edward, as the son of George Duke of Clarence, Richard III's brother, was Henry VII's chief competitor to the throne. He appears from a contemporary reference to have been mentally retarded in 1499. His sister fared better, but was eventually cut down by Henry VIII in 1541.

France, before marrying for love Charles Brandon, Duke of Suffolk. Apart from her first-born, Arthur, who died in his fifteenth year, Elizabeth also buried in her lifetime Elizabeth, born in 1492, who died before she was three, and Edmund, born in 1499, who just saw the opening of the new century. Child-bearing seriously undermined the Queen's health; she never recovered from her last confinement and died on her thirty-eighth birthday, in 1503, a day or so before the infant Catherine. Gentle and devout, much in the tradition of the noble ladies of late medieval poetry, her death evoked a moving elegy from Thomas More's pen:

> Adieu! mine own dear spouse, my worthy lord!
> The faithful love, that did us both combine
> In marriage and peaceable concord,
> Into your hands here I do clear resign,
> To be bestowed on your children and mine;
> Erst were ye father, now must ye supply
> The mother's part also, for here I lie.

> Where are our castles now? where are our towers?
> Goodly Richmond, soon art thou gone from me:
> At Westminster, that costly work of yours,
> Mine own dear lord, now shall I never see,
> Almighty God vouchsafe to grant that ye,
> For you and children well may edify;
> My palace builded is, for lo! now here I lie.

There was no role for her in political life, nor did she seek one, for she was essentially the King's wife and the mother of his children.

Honours and rewards had been speedily granted to those who had stood by Henry in exile and fought for him at Bosworth. Pride of place necessarily went to his uncle, Jasper Tudor, who was not only restored to the earldom of Pembroke but created Earl of Bedford. The same day Edward Courtenay became Earl of Devon. In recognition of his father's martyrdom for the Tudor cause, Edward Stafford, aged seven, was restored to the dukedom of Buckingham. Born at Brecon Castle to Catherine Woodville, a sister of Edward IV's Queen, Buckingham seems to have endured much the same kind of hardships

as Henry of Richmond in his earliest days. His mother now married Jasper Tudor, Earl of Bedford, and in consequence he was brought to Court at a tender age, though after an early marriage to Northumberland's daughter he spent much of the year at Thornbury Castle, his great house in Gloucestershire, which he had leave to fortify. His tenants regarded him as a prince in his own right, and indeed Henry seemed to treat him with as much affection as if he were his own son. Years afterwards, under Wolsey's rule, his proud Plantagenet blood would prove his undoing. Unnatural death ran in a macabre fashion in the Staffords, for beyond his own father's execution lay the successive deaths in battle of his grandfather, his great-grand-father and great-great-grandfather.

Thomas, Lord Stanley, the Lady Margaret's husband, who

The north and west fronts of Penshurst Place in Kent. Edward Stafford, Duke of Buckingham, added the three-storeyed structure, known as Buckingham Building, in the centre of the picture.

had played a significant part in Henry's victory, became Earl of Derby and served as Lord High Steward at the coronation. Within the year he was to be chosen, with Oxford, to stand god-father to Prince Arthur. He was as loyal to Henry as his brother, Sir William Stanley, proved treacherous. The King enjoyed staying at Knowsley Hall in Derbyshire where, until the Earl's death, the Lady Margaret principally lived.

Bishop Morton, more than any other individual the architect of Henry's succession, had stayed in Flanders until he was summoned home. Already an old man by fifteenth-century standards, much work lay ahead for him. Within a few months he had succeeded his old master, Bourchier, as Archbishop of Canterbury and was soon afterwards appointed Lord Chancellor. Morton was to die in harness as the century closed – a

LEFT Cardinal Morton's tomb in Canterbury Cathedral. In the arch above his tomb, are carved the various symbols of the Cardinal and his King – including an eagle on a tun, the portcullis of the Beauforts and the Tudor rose surmounted by a crown.

RIGHT The Tudor Gatehouse at Lambeth Palace, which was built by Cardinal Morton in 1490. He made use of the two flanking towers which were already in existence, and built between them the gateways, and on top, the audience chamber and private apartments which he occupied as Archbishop of Canterbury.

cardinal in the great tradition of ecclesiastical statesmen, like Beaufort and Chichele before him. Twice the King's age, he was one of the very few men whom Henry absolutely trusted and he relied on his experience in diplomacy and finance. He used his Church revenues to build Lambeth Palace, Hatfield Manor and the Bell Tower at Canterbury Cathedral. Thomas More was placed in his household as a boy and left a characteristic portrait of him: 'In his face did shine such an amiable reverence as was pleasant to behold; gentle in communication, yet earnest and sage. . . . In the law he had profound knowledge,

45

CLARVS WYNTONIÆ PRÆSVL COGNOIE FOXVS
QVI PIVS HOC OLIM NOBILE STRVXIT OPVS
TALIS ERAT FORMA TALIS DVM VIXIT AMICTV
QVALEM SPECTANTI PICTA TABELLA REFERT.

LEFT Richard Fox, whom
Henry appointed Bishop of
Exeter and Lord Privy
Seal on his accession.
Fox went on to become in
turn, Bishop of Bath and
Wells, of Durham and
finally of Winchester.
The portrait hangs in the
hall of Corpus Christi
College, Oxford, which
Fox founded in the
first decade of the
sixteenth century.

in wit he was incomparable and in memory excellent. These qualities which in him were by nature singular, he by learning and use had made perfect.'

Richard Fox, who had been Morton's chief coadjutor in exile, was now appointed Bishop of Exeter and, after a brief spell as Secretary, became Lord Privy Seal. Realising that affairs of State would leave him little time for diocesan duties, he at once installed a suffragan. In swift succession he exchanged one bishopric for another, as a richer see became vacant – Bath and Wells, Durham (from which he played a notable part in the improvement of relations with Scotland) and finally Winchester. After Morton's death, Fox had to bear the brunt of diplomacy single-handed. It is to Richard Fox rather than to Archbishop Morton that the tale of the 'heads I win, tails you lose' attitude of King Henry's ministers to taxation should properly be ascribed. Cardinal Morton, according to Francis Bacon's *History*, was the inventor of the eponymous fork: 'the sparing were to be pressed for money because they saved, the lavish because they spent', but Thomas More told Erasmus, fifty years before Bacon was born, that when Fox had been appointed commissioner for raising a loan from the clergy, he remarked to the well-dressed that they displayed their ability to pay and to the meanly clad that they must be hoarding money and could spare the King some of it.

The King's Secretary was Oliver King, a civil lawyer, who climbed the ladder of clerical promotion immediately behind Richard Fox. He had served Edward IV but had been dismissed from the secretaryship by Richard III. Busy at Court, he never set foot in his Exeter diocese and it was not until his fourth year as Bishop of Bath and Wells that he paid his first visit to Bath, where the abbey church was in a ruinous state. That night he had a dream as remarkable as Jacob's, he said, which he interpreted as a divine command to rebuild Bath Abbey. This he achieved and on the stonework of the west front is depicted an incident from his dream, with angels descending ladders from heaven and the apposite verse from the Book of Judges, 'Trees going to choose their King said "Be to us the Olive King".'

One last reward for notable service to Henry's cause by a cleric is worth noticing, for Christopher Urswick, the Lady Margaret's chaplain and Morton's secret agent, soon found

OPPOSITE Lady Margaret
Beaufort, Countess of
Richmond and Derby, and
Henry VII's mother, at her
prayers. The portcullis of
the Beauforts and Tudor
rose have been
incorporated into the
canopy above and behind
her. This painting now
hangs in St John's College,
Cambridge, which Lady
Margaret founded in 1509.

himself a prebendary of St Paul's and Master of the King's Hall,
Cambridge. Henry, sure of his discretion, used him on embassies
and his ability was further rewarded by his appointment in turn
as Dean of York and Dean of Windsor, where he left his mark
as a builder.

A number of laymen prominent at Court were in fact second
generation servants of the Crown. Giles Daubeney's father had
been a Knight of the Body under Edward IV; the father of Sir
Richard Guildford had been Controller of the Household of
the same King, while Sir Reginald Bray's father had sat at
Henry VI's Council table. There was in effect greater con-
tinuity in personnel between the Yorkist and Tudor govern-
ments than is often realised, and in many cases the great divide
was not Bosworth Field but Richard's usurpation. Henry was
able to build on the administrative and financial reforms of
Edward IV so successfully that he appeared as a new-style
monarch, served by new men, whereas, as we shall see, he was
reluctant to be an innovator.

Richard Guildford had come over to Henry in 1483 in Brittany, had landed with him at Milford Haven and fought at
Bosworth. Such loyalty had won him a seat in Council and the
post of Master of the Ordnance. A man of parts, he also served
Henry afloat and, where Kent and Sussex meet, he pioneered
the reclamation of land from the sea; 'Guildford Level' keeps
his name green. In 1506 Sir Richard was to make a pilgrimage
to the Holy Land in the company of the Prior of Gisbourn, and
though they soon reached Jaffa, they had much trouble in
persuading the Mamelukes to allow them to proceed to
Jerusalem. In the eyes of the Church their pilgrimage was
crowned with success, for they died in the Holy City on successive days. Richard's widow was a sister of Sir Nicholas Vaux
of Harrowden, whose father had been a zealous Lancastrian.
The son had been brought up in the Lady Margaret's household,
which gave him a passport to royal service and he was knighted
after the battle of Stoke and appointed Lieutenant of Guisnes
Castle. Sir Nicholas was easily identified at Court for he had a
penchant for flamboyant clothes; in his native Northamptonshire he was a progressive farmer and a great encloser of
common land.

Reginald Bray had begun his career as steward in the house-

hold of Sir Henry Stafford, the second husband of the Countess of Richmond, and he stayed in her service after Stafford's death when she married Lord Stanley. As we have noticed, Morton used Bray as a confidential agent in the negotiations leading to the exiled Tudor's announcement that he would marry Elizabeth of York. At Henry's coronation he was dubbed a Knight of the Bath and soon afterwards became High Steward of Oxford University. Bray was most concerned in his later years with building ventures and if he was not responsible for the design of the Henry VII Chapel at Westminster (with which he was once credited), he jointly laid its foundation stone with Abbot Islip in 1503. He was also much occupied with the King's Works at St George's, Windsor, and is buried in a Chapel in the south aisle which he had planned himself in detail.

Giles Daubeney, who had fled to Brittany on the failure of Buckingham's rebellion in 1483 and was attainted, triumphed with Henry. He became a Privy Councillor and from the accession held the offices of Master of the Mint, Master of the Hart Hounds and Lieutenant of Calais; the next year he received a barony. Henry used him on embassies and relied on his military experience – notably in putting down Warbeck's second rebellion. Later he became Lord Chamberlain, and his unflinching loyalty to his master earned him a vault in Westminster Abbey. Lord Daubeney had married Elizabeth, the daughter of Sir John Arundel, whose other daughter had married Sir Henry Marney. Like Daubeney, Marney became a Councillor, fought at the battles of Stoke and Blackheath and acquired a peerage. His fine classical tomb in the church of his native Layer Marney in Essex, is an early example of a style of funeral monument that was to become common as Renaissance craftsmanship permeated England in the next half-century.

The 'new men' proper in the royal service were Richard Empson and Edmund Dudley, who came to the fore in the later years of the reign. Their disgrace after Henry VIII's accession, culminating in their being hounded to death as traitors for extortionate actions, led men to denigrate their origins. Empson, they said, was son of a sieve-maker from Towcester, and Dudley the heir of a Sussex carpenter. Each possessed ability which the King was quick to recognise; each had risen through the law to become in turn Speaker of the Commons and from

OPPOSITE Sir Reginald Bray portrayed in a stained glass window at Malvern Priory.

ELIZABETHA · VXOR
HENRICI · VII

there it was a short step to the Council and high office. Their activities as Henry's chief tax-gatherers in the new century are discussed below (pp. 188–9).

In the spring of 1486 Henry left Elizabeth behind at Greenwich while he went on a lengthy progress of the eastern counties, Lincoln and Yorkshire, to show himself to his subjects in areas which had been predominantly Yorkist. By a show of regal pomp and deft use of propaganda in the civic receptions on the route, he intended to take the heart out of disaffection in regions where men had followed their leaders in standing by 'the White Rose'. The Earl of Surrey, head of the House of Howard, was safely in the Tower and his East Anglian estates in the King's hands; the Earl of Lincoln, though his wings had been clipped, appeared reconciled to the new regime, but Yorkshire remained uncertain in its loyalties. Henry kept Easter at Lincoln, and while still in the city heard that Lord Lovell and the brothers Humphrey and Thomas Stafford had left their sanctuary in Colchester Abbey, in which they had lain low since Bosworth, and in league with men in York, were gathering an army to oppose Henry. Yet the 'great band of rude and rustical people' which the Staffords had raised in Worcestershire melted away, for the King gained a tactical victory by declaring that all rebels who laid down their arms forthwith would be pardoned. The leaders again escaped – Lovell to friends in Lancashire, the Staffords to sanctuary at Abingdon Abbey. Henry had had enough of traitors abusing the privileged position of the Church and demanded that the brothers be surrendered. When Abbot Sante refused, they were dragged from the Abbey and put in the Tower. Humphrey Stafford, the elder brother, was later executed as an example to potential rebels.

The citizens of York redeemed themselves by their patriotic pageantry, presenting devices showing the double rose of Lancaster and York (including a shower of rose water) and a tableau of the first six Henrys of England proffering a sceptre to Solomon for bestowal on the seventh. While in York, Henry held a Chapter of the Order of the Garter on St George's Day, and having won over Yorkshire he returned south by way of Worcester, Hereford and Bristol, where there were pleas for royal grants to aid ship-building.

OPPOSITE Elizabeth of York, the eldest daughter of Edward IV, and Henry VII's Queen. She is portrayed holding a white rose, the badge of the House of York

After an absence of three months Henry rejoined his Queen in
London and before summer ended they set out with a great
entourage for Winchester, the ancient capital of Saxon England,
where he was determined that the heir of his dynasty should
be born. Here, on 20 September 1486, Elizabeth was delivered
of a son who was named Arthur, 'in honour of the British race'.
The Court poets hailed his birth as inaugurating a golden age
of peace and plenty. Throughout the realm bonfires were lit
as the joyous news arrived – a contrast, indeed, to the unheralded
birth of the father. The baby's christening was postponed a week
while the King and Court awaited the arrival at Winchester of
the Earl of Oxford, principal godfather, who had been delayed
by foul weather. Henry had almost given up hope of Oxford's
appearance and at last ordered the elaborate service to begin,
when word came that the Earl was within a mile of the city and
though he entered the cathedral after the baptism he was in
time to hold the Prince in his arms for Bishop Courtenay to
confirm him. With a male heir, uniting in his person Lancaster
and York, the Tudor line seemed assured.

Just as Henry seemed to be riding on the crest of the wave,
storm clouds arose. News came to him of the existence of a
pretender claiming to be the eleven-year-old Earl of Warwick,
who it was claimed 'had escaped from the Tower'. As 'Warwick' he claimed to be legitimate King of England. Lambert
Simnel, who played this exacting role, was the son of a joiner
and organ-maker in Oxford, and had been selected as Warwick's impersonator by William Seymour, a priest who had
dreamed that he was tutor to a king. Simnel was the right age
and stature for the part and was methodically schooled to act
it. Once Simnel was crowned 'Edward VI', Symonds could
become his Archbishop Morton. Few could remember exactly
what the real Warwick looked like, for he had been in prison
since the accession. A lad decked out in clothes befitting the
premier Earl of England could easily take in many people in
days when pictorial likenesses were non-existent. Most of
Simnel's supporters were convinced that he was Warwick while
the few in the secret, such as Francis Lovell, were satisfied that
he was the meetest instrument for overthrowing Henry.

The way in which men rallied to the pretender showed how
insecure was Henry's hold on his kingdom. To quash rumours

about the counterfeit Warwick, the real Earl was taken out of
the Tower to attend High Mass in St Paul's while Convocation
was in session, and opportunity was given for Councillors and
others to talk with the boy. Lincoln was now convinced that
the prisoner was indeed his own cousin and that the hope of the
Yorkists lay in mounting a campaign with foreign aid to fight
for the impostor as the surest way of toppling Henry Tudor.

55

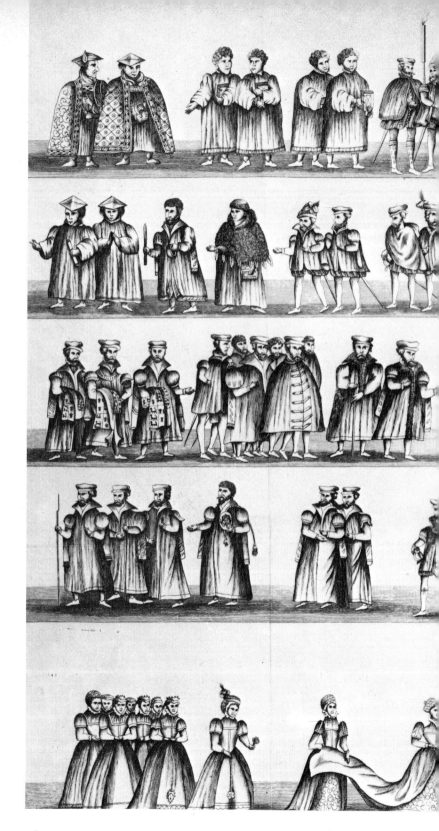

A late sixteenth-century engraving of the procession to the christening of Arthur, eldest son of Henry VII and Elizabeth of York, which took place in Winchester Cathedral in September 1486.

A *grisaille* miniature of Margaret, Dowager Duchess of Burgundy at prayer. Margaret, the sister of Edward IV, married Charles the Bold in 1468. She became an implacable enemy of Henry VII, and supported and encouraged the rebellions of Lambert Simnel and Perkin Warbeck. (Bodleian Ms Douce 365 f. cxv)

Simnel could be cast aside either for the real Warwick, if he was still alive, or for Lincoln himself. There was enough Plantagenet blood to 'give the King's grace a breakfast'. With the support of Margaret of Burgundy, sister of Edward IV and Richard III, who remained an implacable enemy of Henry, Lincoln and Lovell were able to hire two thousand German mercenaries

58

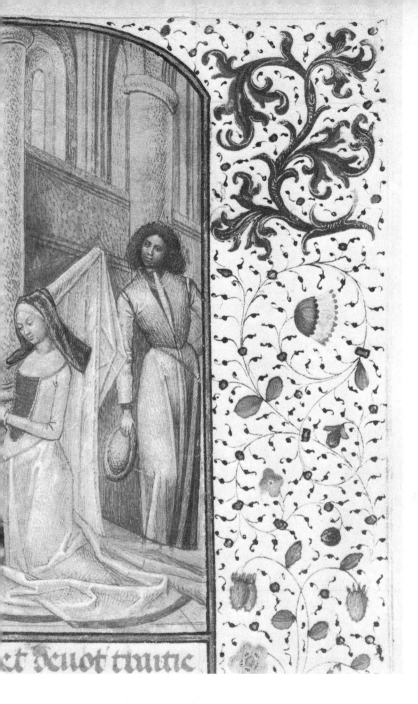

et &euot'tintie

under Martin Schwartz as the backbone of an army. They sailed to Ireland, where dissident landowners led by the Earl of Kildare welcomed them with open arms so that Simnel was crowned 'Edward VI' on Whitsun Day in Dublin Cathedral and was paid homage. Years afterwards Henry mocked a delegation of Irish peers at Westminster, by reminding them of their

59

OPPOSITE Henry VII with his two councillors, Richard Empson and Edmund Dudley. Early in the next reign they were to suffer death for their service to Henry.

folly: 'My Lords of Ireland, you will crown apes at last.' But for the present, with Lincoln's defection, Lambert Simnel's cause was no laughing matter, for the roots of the White Rose were strong.

Henry VII suspected his mother-in-law, Elizabeth Woodville, of being enmeshed in the Yorkist rebellion that gathered round Simnel and he acted swiftly. After his marriage he had restored to her most of her dower lands, and it had been the Queen-Dowager, not the Lady Margaret, who was godmother to Prince Arthur. Now she was in disgrace, though the reasons he gave for his treatment of her were equivocal, for he gave out that she had forfeited her rights to her dower estates by having agreed, three years before, to deliver herself and her daughters to Richard III. Certainly Elizabeth Woodville was a woman of mischievous nature and a useful figurehead for traitors. She would be as well out of the way, so Henry persuaded her to withdraw to Bermondsey Abbey, the religious house to which of custom kings of England could present boarders. Her property was settled on Elizabeth of York and she received a modest pension. Though she still paid occasional visits to Court, it was at Bermondsèy, like Henry's paternal grandmother, Catherine of Valois, that Elizabeth Woodville ended her days in 1492. In accordance with her wishes, she was buried at Windsor beside the coffin of Edward IV.

Lincoln and his supporters landed with their puppet king at Furness on the Lancashire coast with a far larger army than Henry Tudor had brought to Bosworth Field, but he found few recruits on his march to swell the numbers of poorly-armed Irish, and even when they reached Yorkshire the welcome was cool, showing Henry a dividend from his progress of the previous year. 'Their snowball did not gather as it went', wrote Lord Bacon, no doubt because true Englishmen thought it odious 'to have a King brought in to them upon the shoulders of Irish and Dutch.' Henry had gone to Kenilworth as soon as he sensed the danger, for it was roughly in the centre of England, and was a stronghold from which he could move against the invaders whichever route they might take, and his intelligence service was effective. The rebels turned south, marching through Sherwood Forest, hoping to take Newark, with its stout castle, and forded the River Trent at Fiskerton Ferry, to

the south-east of Newark. As the royal army advanced along the Fosse Way, Lincoln positioned his men on the slopes of the hill near the village of Stoke, which centuries later was to become famous as a pottery town. On the morning of 16 June he threw his troops against Henry's vanguard, led as at Bosworth by Oxford. He held this weighty attack with difficulty, but soon reinforcements from Henry's main army were on the scene and after fierce fighting the Tudor dynasty survived its most serious threat. Henry lost two thousand men, the rebels twice that number, including the mercenary leader Schwartz, Lincoln himself, Sir Thomas Broughton from Lancashire and Fitzgerald, Lord Chancellor of Ireland. Francis Lovell tried to escape but was probably drowned with his horse trying to swim the Trent. Henry had hoped to take Lincoln alive to learn from him the ramifications of the rising at home and abroad, but the prize captive of the Battle of Stoke was the pretender himself, who received unexpected clemency. With a bizarre touch Henry put Simnel to work as the most menial of servants in the royal kitchens, turning the spit. Later he was promoted to become a falconer, and long after the White Rose party in England had withered away he died peacefully in his bed. There is good reason for reckoning Stoke a more decisive battle than Bosworth Field, yet Henry by no means regarded its outcome as a foregone conclusion. He had no standing army, no professional mercenaries. Lincoln's treachery made him even less trusting of men and he would be haunted for years to come by the fear that councillors might conspire to succeed where the 'Dark Earl' had failed; yet in the middle of 1487 Henry could outwardly appear confident – he was no longer a political adventurer, but a King recognised by his fellow sovereigns abroad.

Despite the fact that the illustrious Houses of Lancaster and York had been united, so that Prince Arthur was equally the heir of each, Henry VII did not forget his own Lancastrian heritage and he wanted to glorify the name of Henry VI, the martyred King who had prophesied his own triumphant rule. Papal recognition of Henry VI's sanctity was sought by a claim for canonisation. The negotiations with Rome, involving tests of evidence submitted about Henry's miracles, proceeded slowly; nothing had been decided by 1509. The King had

RIGHT The alms box set up by Henry VII at the tomb of Henry VI in St George's Chapel, Windsor. Pilgrims visiting the tomb placed their offerings in one of its many slots.

wanted his body to be removed to Westminster, where he was making elaborate plans to enlarge and beautify the Abbey, and to make way for a Henry VI Chapel to house the shrine. The Lady Chapel behind the High Altar was demolished and – an appropriate touch – 'The White Rose' tavern next to it was pulled down. Because of the income which a religious foundation could expect from the offerings at shrines, there was an unseemly dispute between Windsor, Chertsey Abbey and the monks of Westminster over the custody of the relics. In the end Henry VI's coffin remained at Windsor.

Henry was equally aware of the importance of recognising his Welsh heritage. A century after Bosworth Field a Welsh antiquarian lauded him as 'a Moses who delivered us from our bondage'. Such was a rose-tinted view of the past, for in Henry's actual reign some, who had been swayed by the Anglophobia of the bards in their propaganda to raise supporters for Richmond's cause when an exile, now complained that there was no vengeance meted out to the English foe, as had been promised. Henry certainly rewarded his countrymen who had aided his victory, but this was largely by entrusting them with minor posts in the government of Wales and in bringing some of them to Court. There were now Welshmen among the yeomen of the guard – including Lord Burghley's grandfather – a few secured posts in the Chamber and two of the Esquires for the Body were somewhat distant kinsmen of the King from Pennydd in Anglesey. Soon a certain Edward ap Rice was granted a brewhouse in Fleet Street appropriately called 'The Welshman'. Initially the government of South Wales could be safely left to the King's uncle Jasper, Earl of Bedford, and when he died without heirs his extensive chain of lordships – Pembroke, Glamorgan, Newport, Abergavenny and the rest – reverted to the Crown. The stalwart of the 1485 campaign, Rhys ap Thomas of Dynevor, was given the Garter at Bosworth and subsequently became appointed Justice and Chamberlain of South Wales. Henry warmly addressed him as 'Father Rhys', but he kept him in his place, for there were to be no more troublesome Marcher lordships which had so weakened the Crown during the civil wars.

To regain royal power in the Principality which had been so eroded during the years of strife Henry revived the Council of

ABOVE Catherine of Aragon as a young girl, from her portrait by Michel Sittow. This picture tallies closely with the contemporary descriptions of the Princess at the time of her arrival in England.

LEFT Arthur, Prince of Wales, Henry VII's eldest son and heir to the throne. This portrait was probably painted just before his death in April 1502.

the Marches, first appointed by Edward IV, and enlarged its jurisdiction; there, as in England, the first Tudor was the traditionalist concerned to make an existing system work rather than to undertake root and branch reforms in administration. To give the Welsh people pride in his dynasty, he created Arthur Prince of Wales in November 1489. After Arthur's marriage twelve years later, he and his wife, Princess Catherine, went to keep their little Court at Ludlow Castle, guided by Sir Reginald Bray, for a pathetically brief tour of duty, as it happened. New men came to pay homage – Griffiths from the north, Vaughans and Herberts from the south-east who were to found county families that proved the mainstay of Tudor rule. There was to be no vengeance on the English because Henry had become an English King in outlook. In his last years he granted a remarkable series of new charters to the royal lordships, such as Bromfield and Yale in Denbighshire, which brought local custom much more into line with English practice and started a process which was to be continued by the Act of 1536 for incorporating Wales within the administration and law of England.

3
Diplomacy and Sedition 1485-1502

THE EUROPE THAT HENRY had known for most of his years
of exile was changing fast. Louis XI, who with deft diplomacy had extended the frontiers of France by conquering the
duchy of Burgundy and bringing Provence, Anjou, Picardy
and all the other independent fiefs, save Brittany, under his
rule, had died before Henry's accession. His daughter, Anne of
Beaujeu, acted with her husband as regent during the minority
of her brother Charles VIII who, once the Breton question was
settled, would plunder the Italian states. The Habsburg Holy
Roman Emperor, Frederick III, had ruled ineffectively since
1452 but now withdrew to Linz to spend his last days studying
astronomy and alchemy, while his son Maximilian, King of the
Romans, an able and astute politician, took over the government in Vienna in preparation for his election as Emperor in
1493. The old man had become so obsessed with the idea of his
family's future greatness that he devised the monogram
A.E.I.O.U. (*Austriae est imperare orbi universo* – Austria is destined
to rule the whole world) and his vision seemed answered by
his son's marriage to Mary of Burgundy, the heiress to Flanders
– a buffer state bustling with activity all along the waterways
leading to the great port of Antwerp, which already dominated
England's overseas trade.

Spain, like France, had become a more unified state following
the marriage of Ferdinand of Aragon and Isabella of Castile and
their subsequent expulsion of the Moors from the peninsula.
Another marriage of tremendous significance was that of their
daughter Joanna of Castile to Maximilian's son, Philip of
Burgundy, in 1496. If the corruption of the Papacy under Innocent VIII seemed a byword, worse was to follow, for the
scandalous election of Alexander VI as Pope in 1492 established
the rule of his family, the Borgias, in central Italy. Alexander's
son, Cesare Borgia, became an archbishop at sixteen, his
daughter, Lucrezia, changed husbands to suit shifts of policy
in extending the Pope's temporal power. Poisoning became a
standard political weapon, so that the Borgias could subdue the
rival Houses of Orsini and Colonna in Rome with a ruthless
disregard for morality and public opinion which no temporal
ruler could have followed. If, as Polydore Vergil maintained,
the judicial murder of the Earl of Warwick in 1499 gave
Henry VII many sleepless nights, Pope Alexander VI would have

68

found such squeamish twinges of conscience a ridiculous trait in a king. Nearer home, the fate of James III of Scotland was a warning, for he fell in battle against his rebellious nobles; his thirteen-year-old son, succeeding as James IV, looked to the Auld Alliance with France to embarrass England on the borders and was to shelter the pretender Perkin Warbeck. Henry Tudor had need of all his native cunning in pitting himself against the wily leaders of the new Europe who would exploit his every weakness. He desperately wanted to be acknowledged by other princes, without seeing England drawn into their endemic warfare.

ABOVE Triumphal car carrying the figures of Maximilian I and Mary of Burgundy, which formed part of a procession to celebrate Maximilian's inheritance of the duchy of Burgundy: woodcut by Albrecht Dürer.

69

His first venture was to render modest aid to his former host, Francis II of Brittany, whose duchy was being threatened by France in the summer of 1488. It was rather more than a gallant gesture, since Henry feared that, if an over-mighty France controlled the hitherto independent Breton coast, England would lose her command of the Channel; moreover, under the Paris-Edinburgh axis every French success weakened England's position on her northern border. In answer to Brittany's plea, Henry sent three vessels and a company of volunteers under Lord Scales, uncle to Queen Elizabeth. But Duke Francis soon had to accept terms with the Regents of France, placing himself as a vassal of Charles VIII and pledging that his daughter and heiress, Anne, should not marry without his consent. Next month the old Duke died and Charles at once demanded Anne's wardship. When Parliament met, Henry asked for supplies for war and there were not a few Englishmen who hoped that he would renew the Hundred Years' War to regain English possessions in Normandy and Gascony. Under a treaty with Anne of Brittany, signed at Radon early in 1489, Henry again sent an army to the duchy. At the same time he found further allies in the Archduke Maximilian of Burgundy and in Ferdinand and Isabella of Spain, who were anxious to lay their hands on the French possessions of Roussillon and Cerdagne, near the Pyrenees. The Treaty of Dordrecht with Burgundy renewed the old accord between England and the Netherlands which had been overturned by the Dowager Duchess's active support of her native House of York; the corresponding Treaty of Medina del Campo with Spain looked forward from a mere political alliance to a marriage between the Houses of Tudor and Aragon.

Henry was, however, hampered in executing his plans for the Breton expedition, since war taxation had provoked a rebellion in Yorkshire, where a mob had slain the Earl of Northumberland. The English garrison at Calais rendered great service to Henry's Burgundian ally in rescuing his troops at Dixmunde from Flemish rebels, but suddenly Maximilian signed a separate peace with France, leaving England high and dry. Henry might also have made peace himself, but the Francophobe representatives from the shires and boroughs had not voted generous supplies for a minimal expedition. When

the King told Parliament that French offers to treat were quite inadequate, the Commons cheerfully assented to further taxes, and it was clear to him that he must prepare for a vigorous campaign, especially since Anne, weakened by factions in the duchy, had been forced to accept Charles VIII's proposal of marriage, so that effectively Brittany had become annexed to the kingdom of France. Henry finally left Sandwich for Calais in October 1492 with an army of twenty-five thousand foot-soldiers and sixteen hundred horsemen under the Earl of Oxford, and began the siege of Boulogne. A show of force proved sufficient, for after a mere nine days Charles VIII, no longer subject to a council of Regency, offered Henry attractive terms, which were signed at Étaples. He was to be reimbursed for his expenses in the Breton campaigns and, more significant, was to receive the arrears of the pension granted to Edward IV, by a treaty in 1475, which amounted to some £5,000 a year. This was a successful deal, for Henry was not by nature a warrior, even though there was bound to be criticism from the bellicose that he had negotiated too soon. It was enemies threatening his crown at home, rather than foreign foes, to whom Henry would never show quarter. He had learned a lesson, too, about perfidious allies, for besides Maximilian's early withdrawal from the coalition, Ferdinand made it plain he had no need of an English alliance once he had gained the little mountain principalities. But for Charles VIII's invasion of Italy in 1494, which was to alter the whole balance of power in Europe, Henry Tudor would have remained under the shadow of attack from the Continental powers who, as it was, were eager to exploit every twitch of disaffection in England.

In the autumn of 1491, a Breton merchant named Pregent Meno sailed into Cork harbour with a consignment of silks and other fineries. Among his crew was a youth of seventeen whom he employed to show off his wares – Master Perkin Warbeck (or Osbeck) from Tournai, who was the son of a boatman on the Scheldt. The men of Cork, seeing Perkin clad in his master's choicest goods, detected a royal bearing; the mayor was sure he must be the Earl of Warwick, others that he was the younger brother of Edward V, Prince Richard of York, and it was agreed that the lad should take on the identity of the latter. Denials were useless, for the chief citizens of Cork were adamant, 'and so, against my will', said the victim years afterwards, 'they made me to learn English and taught me what I should do and say'. Though Kildare was not to be taken in, numbers of the Irish, led by the Earl of Desmond, had remembered nothing from the lesson of Simnel five years back. Soon there was support for the pretender from the Kings of France and Scotland, from Margaret of Burgundy and the Emperor Maximilian, all anxious to fish in Henry Tudor's troubled waters.

Henry was not to be rid of the impostor for six years. At first he made derisory comments about 'this lad who calls himself Plantagenet', but when other sovereigns claimed to be convinced of Perkin's royal birth, saying that they were satisfied with his identity from birthmarks, even the King of England began to have doubts, for the bodies of the princes in the Tower had never been found. Eventually his agents uncovered the truth about Perkin, but not before latent Yorkist sympathy had rallied to his cause in England.

When Margaret of Burgundy refused to bow to Henry's demands to surrender 'the exiled Duke of York', Henry severed commercial relations with Flanders for a full two years, even though the effects on English overseas trade were disastrous. The impostor hobnobbed with the Emperor Maximilian, who fêted him as 'King of England' and assigned him a personal bodyguard wearing the livery of the White Rose. Fortunately for Henry, the ambitions of Charles VIII of France to conquer Naples and make himself the dominant power in Italy ushered in sixty years of Habsburg–Valois rivalry and thus Warbeck's principal supporters were distracted; the states of Renaissance Italy were worth ten times the attention that the pretender expected to be lavished on him. Charles's Italian adventures gave Henry a breathing-space to inquire minutely into potential support for Perkin in England and he bribed Sir Robert Clifford, who was well acquainted with the Burgundian Court, to name suspects. Once he had sufficient information, Henry pounced, early in 1495. Among those arrested were Dean Worsley of St Paul's, Lord Fitzwalter, who had been Steward of the Royal Household, and most serious of all, Sir William Stanley, without whose aid the King might not have been

'This lad who calls himself Plantagenet'

73

victorious at Bosworth. Henry could hardly credit this information, incriminating the younger brother of his mother's husband, the man whom he met almost daily as Lord Chamberlain. This was far worse than Lincoln's treachery at Stoke and Henry realised that for a decade he had been harbouring a viper in his bosom. Whom, then, could he trust?

Certainly the evidence against Sir William Stanley was imperfect; at most he seems to have hinted that if Warbeck were indeed the true son of Edward IV, he would not take up arms against him. This was perhaps no more than taking out insurance cover against another Yorkist restoration, for Stanley had become a wealthy man through his service to Henry and had more to lose than most if the Tudor monarchy fell. But the King was in no mood to weigh Stanley's qualifying words and construed the drift of his remarks as being constructive treason. He was executed on 16 February as an example to others.

State trials and executions took the heart out of Yorkist disaffection and Perkin's supporters seemed as 'sand without lime', though the pretender refused to give up hope. Both Margaret of Burgundy and the Emperor Maximilian thought it would be imprudent to deprive him of modest financial support and if his was a thoroughly risky enterprise no one doubted that the stakes were high. For ready cash, Perkin was prepared to sign away areas of his future kingdom. Margaret was to receive from her 'nephew' the town and castle of Scarborough, while Maximilian and his son Philip were assigned the reversion of 'the Duke of York's' rights to England, France, Wales and Ireland if he died without a male heir. An expedition was prepared for invading England, comprising largely of adventurers and low-grade mercenaries. Warbeck anchored off Deal in July 1495 and sent an advance party ashore to spy out the land. The men of Kent had been alerted to the possibility of an invasion, for Henry had to rely on volunteers near the coast since he had no regular army; and when the Yorkist banners were seen the strangers were challenged. 'We belong to the Duke of York', came the answer. The challenger, completely outnumbered, acted the part of a sympathiser; 'We seek no other lord in the world. We will live and die with him. Let him and his company put ashore and we will do him all possible honour, aid and glory.' By the ruse of offering to fetch ale for the

LEOPHAS FRATER CARNALIS IO-
EPHI MARITI DIVAE VIRG MARIAE

I
IACOBVS MINOR EPVS MARIA CLEOPHAE SORO
HIEROSOLIMITANVS VIRG MAR PVTATIVA MA
TERTERA D N

III   II
IOSEPH IVSTVS SIMON ZELOTES CONSO
BRINVS DNI NRI

Pierre Warbeck natif de Tournay supposé pour Richard
Duc d'Yorck second fils d'Edouard IV. Roy d'Angleterre l'an 1492.
fut pendu à Londres sur la fin de l'an 1499

invaders, he called up enough men to overpower them so that one hundred and fifty were slain and most of the rest taken prisoner, the foreigners to be ransomed, the English to be hanged. The pretender and his main force slipped their cables to sail westward and by the end of July they had joined the Earl of Desmond in Munster.

When Henry read the report of the sheriff of Kent, he must have looked back to his own experiences in 1483 when he had sailed from Brittany to Poole and then to Plymouth. He was less anxious now that Warbeck had turned to Ireland instead of returning to his protectors in the Netherlands, for although Ireland had rallied to Simnel and given Warbeck his initial backing, the King had already sent as Lord Deputy one of his ablest men, Sir Edward Poynings, in whom he had complete confidence. With eleven ships, the pretender sailed into Waterford harbour to attack the town by land and water, yet he met with fierce resistance. Before long Poynings was on the scene with a considerable force to raise the siege of Waterford, and Warbeck's army melted away.

The next that Henry heard of the pretender was that he had sailed to Scotland and been royally welcomed by James IV at Stirling. This seemed an alarming development, for Henry was anxious for a lasting peace with Scotland and had already sent envoys to Edinburgh to treat for a marriage between his elder daughter, Margaret, and the King. He summoned Parliament in October and used it to proffer an olive branch to former supporters of Richard III, still proscribed, to wean them from throwing in their lot with Perkin. After ten years of rule he could afford a show of magnanimity. The *De Facto* Act, which Parliament passed, declared that no person assisting the reigning King of England against his enemies should be liable to impeachment or attainder, though any subject who in the future deserted Henry would naturally enough be excluded from such a benefit. At the same time Henry had the acts of attainder against the Earl of Kildare and various smaller fry annulled.

For James IV, with his eyes on the border country and beyond, the presence at his Court of 'Prince Richard of England' (as he called him) was a godsend. He gave tournaments in his honour and married him to his cousin, Lady Catherine Gordon, the

OPPOSITE Perkin Warbeck, the son of a boatman on the Scheldt who claimed to be Richard, Duke of York, the younger of the ill-fated Princes in the Tower. His rebellions caused Henry great problems until he was executed in 1499. Drawing from the *Recueil d'Arras*.

daughter of the Earl of Huntly, and a great beauty. James prepared for war with England and had wrung from Warbeck a promise of fifty thousand marks and the stronghold of Berwick-on-Tweed once he became King of England. Yet no more than fourteen hundred Scots could be mustered for the invasion and most of them were bent on settling personal scores with men across the Border, burning and looting in the traditional way, rather than in fighting for a dubious adventurer's claim to a foreign kingdom. The large-scale invasion of September 1496 degenerated into a border campaign. James IV himself rode no more than four miles into Henry's realm, for as soon as Lord Neville arrived with four thousand men he retired in haste across the River Tweed.

Since James had broken the peace, Henry was determined to humble him and force him to surrender the pretender; if this could be achieved by diplomatic means, so well and good, otherwise he would resort to war. The possibility of war made an unanswerable case for heavy taxes, and at a much-enlarged Council held at Westminster, representatives of the principal boroughs as well as of the shires, the temporal peers and bishops undertook that when Parliament met in January it would grant an unprecedented sum for Henry to pursue a vigorous Scottish campaign. With this assurance, the King felt entitled to arrange forced loans from the wealthiest communities. From London, for instance, he netted £4,000, though he had demanded as much as £10,000; and nearly £60,000 had come in before Parliament met to hear Cardinal Morton's forceful speech about the King's great need for money to punish the perfidious Scots. Without difficulty the sums were voted and, together with taxes from the clergy, approved by Convocation, would provide him with £160,000.

Throughout England the local commissioners for the subsidy went about their unpopular business while Lord Daubeney raised an army for the North, but in May Henry heard that the men of Cornwall were in arms as a protest against the burdensome taxes. The trouble started in the far west where Michael Joseph, the smith of St Keverne, led his fellows to complain about the severities of the district collector. Soon he was supported by a much more effective demagogue – Thomas Flamank, a lawyer from Bodmin, who played upon the disaffected with great skill; although his father was a commissioner for the tax, he said that Henry's war with the Scots was only an excuse 'to pill and poll the people'. Why, he argued, should the tinners who grubbed under the earth and the smallholders who barely scratched a living from the poor soil of the duchy be 'grounded to powder' for 'a little stir of the Scots soon blown over'? Old lawbooks suggested to Flamank that it was unlawful for the men of Cornwall to have to contribute towards operations on Henry's northern border; this was the same kind of argument as that used by John Hampden against Ship Money in the early seventeenth century. Together Flamank and Joseph succeeded in bringing to their cause fifteen thousand men and they promised to lead them peaceably to London to force King Henry to dismiss his financial experts, Morton and Bray. They were not coming as rebels against the King, said Flamank, but to rescue him from evil advisers; they were no Yorkist mob, but true-born Englishmen. Reaching Taunton, some of their followers tasted blood by killing a collector of the subsidy, and then they marched to Wells, where James Tutchet, Lord Audley, at odds with the King whom he felt undervalued his abilities, was persuaded to command their army. Though the men of Bristol boycotted them, the rebels moved through the West Country unimpeded, with no weapons except bows and farm implements, astounding the citizens of Winchester, who had cheered Arthur's birth, by their successful progress, setting their sights on Kent, the traditional home of protest, which had fathered both Wat Tyler and Jack Cade. On the march they committed no pillage and this helped attract men to them.

Henry returned from Woodstock to find the capital in a panic. He himself had guarded Henley bridge, in case the rebels attempted to cross the Thames there, and Edmund de la Pole, Earl of Suffolk, younger brother of the late Earl of Lincoln, was called out of bed to defend Staines bridge; at all events, Audley's army must be kept to the south of the river. Henry had sent his Queen to the safety of the Tower and she took with her Henry, the true Duke of York, nearly seven years old. Lord Daubeney had been ordered south with his army, while Thomas Howard, Earl of Surrey, had been despatched to Durham to hold the border. Soon Daubeney's men camped in St George's Fields, ready to defend London, as the rebels moved in from Surrey to

'*A little stir of the Scots soon blown over*'

79

Blackheath. The Lord Mayor called out the craft guilds to defend London Bridge and cheer the King as he passed by. Henry had refused the offer of some of the rebels to surrender Lord Audley and Joseph the blacksmith if he would issue a general pardon. Before dawn on 17 June he had sent a force, led by the faithful Oxford, to cut off the rebels' line of retreat to the south, for they had taken up their position to defend the bridge at Deptford Strand. Then he sent in his spearmen under Sir Humphrey Stanley, who found the bridge heavily defended by the Cornish bowmen, but Daubeney brought in the main body of his troops to force a passage across and lead the attack, with no little risk to himself, into the enemy ranks. By noon it was all over, and two thousand Cornishmen lay dead. Audley and Flamank were taken prisoner on the battlefield, while Michael Joseph was seized trying to reach sanctuary with the friars by Greenwich Palace. Once the issue was certain, Henry moved among his men dubbing knights, and then returned to the City over London Bridge to make his thanksgiving at Old St Paul's.

Henry joined his family in the White Tower and on the Monday visited the three rebel leaders in their cells to cross-question them about the origins of the rising; as with his inter-rogations of Simnel he was anxious to get to the bottom of the affair. After trial, all three men were sentenced to death. Lord Audley was paraded through the City streets dressed in a coat of paper, painted with his arms reversed, before his beheading on Tower Hill. Flamank, the lawyer, did not question the law-fulness of his sentence, but Joseph to the end boasted of his actions which would earn him a niche in the annals of England – 'a fame perpetual and immortal'. Satisfied from his personal investigations that the rank and file of the rebels had sheepishly followed the demagogues, Henry spared the lives of all the others on condition that they speedily departed to their homes, but they would be heavily fined before they received full par-dons. The fines on individuals and communities realised some £14,700 which, to Henry's satisfaction, exceeded by £1,500 his costs both in suppressing the rebellion and in dealing with Warbeck in the weeks which followed.

Henry sent Fox, now Bishop of Durham, and William Warham, Bishop of London, to James IV early in July to nego-tiate afresh about the surrender of Warbeck. By their instructions they were to urge the King, if he refused to deliver the pretender, to send a formal embassy for peace to England and later to come south to meet Henry in person. But before the ambassadors reached the Scottish Court, James had already sent Perkin on his way, to strike in the West Country while the iron was hot. James had lent him a ship and arranged for an escort of two pirates of renown, Andrew and Robert Barton. He would launch a new attack across the border while Warbeck was rallying his English well-wishers; but the timing went wrong almost from the start. Warbeck decided to revisit Cork, where his pseudo-royal career had begun, to muster the Irish Yorkists, yet he did not in fact reach Cork until five weeks after Audley's rebels had been vanquished at Blackheath. Moreover, the one Irishman who might have helped his cause, Sir James Ormond, had just been killed in a brawl. Perkin escaped from Ireland in the nick of time to make for Cornwall, pursued much of the way by four vessels from Waterford, and he landed at Whitesand Bay on 7 September.

A month previously James IV had sent his light horsemen to raid the border and himself began the siege of Norham Castle. His success, however, was no better than in the previous September, for the Earl of Surrey hastened from Yorkshire with twenty thousand men to take the King of Scots completely by surprise; he retreated north and during the rout Surrey's cannon forced the garrison of Ayrton Castle to surrender. It was at Ayrton on the morrow of Michaelmas that, through the agency of the Spanish ambassador, Don Pedro de Ayala, a seven-year truce was signed. Henry had spent only £47,000 out of the £160,000 voted for the campaign.

Henry had received excellent intelligence from Ireland about Warbeck's plans and despite the awkwardness of having to fight on two fronts, made his dispositions with confidence. Daubeney was despatched west to command the levies raised by Buckingham in Gloucestershire, by Sir Rhys ap Thomas in South Wales and by loyalists in Wiltshire, Somerset and Dorset. The Earl of Devon was to hold Exeter, while Henry gathered his main army at Woodstock. Warbeck had left his Scottish wife at St Michael's Mount, to march to Bodmin where he had himself proclaimed Richard IV and was able, despite the collapse of the Cornish rebellion, to attract three thousand men to his

Early sixteenth-century Flemish tapestry now in Magdalen College, Oxford, showing the betrothal of Arthur, Prince of Wales and Catherine of Aragon. Richard Mayhew, President of the College from 1480 to 1506, acted as one of the envoys sent to meet the Spanish Princess when she arrived in England in 1501.

82

banners. Within ten days of landing he was outside the walls of Exeter and though some of his men managed to force the east gate, they were driven back after close hand-to-hand fighting. Next day the rebels gave up their attempt at Exeter and made for Taunton. Warbeck heard with horror that Daubeney's army was already at Glastonbury, twenty miles away, and his courage failed him. Slipping away at night with the 'chief officials of his court', he hoped to find a ship in Southampton Water, but the whole coast was closely guarded and so he took sanctuary in Beaulieu Abbey. Warbeck soon realised that his hiding-place was an open secret and decided it would be prudent to throw himself on the King's mercy.

Henry at last set eyes on the pretender, who had troubled him for so long, at Taunton on 5 October. By then those Cornishmen who had not given up all hope when their leaders deserted had been rounded up. Perkin and his wife were sent under guard to London while Henry proceeded to Exeter to celebrate his victory. He chose to stay at the Treasurer's house in the Close and, in order to have an uninterrupted view of the host of rebels, with halters round their necks, who came to beg for mercy, he commanded a number of trees in front of the house to be felled. At the end of November the pretender repeated his fulsome confession before the greatest in the land and since, as a foreigner, he was not technically guilty of high treason, Henry was prepared to deal leniently with him. He was not put in the Tower, though he was required to reside at Court, while his wife, resuming her maiden name of Lady Catherine Gordon, was placed in Queen Elizabeth's household. After some months on parole, Warbeck had had enough of Henry's mocking clemency and escaped from Westminster Palace. He was taken after a night in Sheen Priory and since he had abused lenient treatment he was sent to the Tower of London, where 'he sees neither sun nor moon'. In August 1499 a madcap conspiracy was hatched involving the escape of Warbeck, the young Warwick and other Yorkists from the Tower, to raise once more the standard of the White Rose. It is impossible to unravel the threads of this affair, which could well have been twisted by an *agent provocateur*, but it is fair to deduce that Perkin once more grasped at another chance of liberty, while the Earl of Warwick, feeble-minded and unable to comprehend the facts, was an innocent

'He sees neither sun nor moon'

84

victim of circumstance. Henry considered that clemency had gone too far and this time Perkin Warbeck was executed. The true Warwick, a close prisoner since the accession, suffered the like fate, and it is hard to acquit Henry of the charge of judicial murder, for Warwick's only crime was his Yorkist blood, and the *De Facto* Act had made all the difference. But for Henry Tudor the safety of the State was the supreme law and he could not believe that Warwick could possibly be innocent of treacherous intrigue, so the Earl went to the gallows at Tyburn. At last Henry could feel safe from potential rivals, and the Spanish sovereigns seeing him as unquestioned master of his realm consented to their daughter Catherine's voyage to England to marry Arthur. Another marriage was in the air, for Lady Catherine Gordon soon became the wife of James Strangeways, a gentleman of the Chamber, and she was destined to acquire two further husbands in swift succession.

Years before, when Henry had defeated Lincoln's rebels at Stoke, he turned his mind to the long-term consolidation of his regime. Thus in March 1488, after feelers had been put out by Ferdinand and Isabella, he empowered Bishop Fox and Giles Daubeney to treat with Spain for an alliance that should include a marriage treaty for affiancing his infant son to Princess Catherine of Aragon. Catherine was the youngest of the five children of Ferdinand and Isabella. The eldest child, an Isabella like her mother, married Alfonso of Portugal, and on his premature death the dynastic politics of the peninsula demanded that she marry his brother and successor, Manuel. Within weeks of Isabella's own death, the next sister, Maria, married Manuel. Joanna, the third child – 'mad Joanna' as she would feature in the chronicles of the times – became the wife of the Habsburg Philip of Burgundy, son of the Emperor Maximilian and Margaret of Burgundy. In contrast to her brother and sisters, Joanna produced a large, healthy brood of children, headed by Charles of Ghent, who one day would rule a united Spain, the Netherlands and the extensive Habsburg lands in Central Europe as well as a vast empire in the New World as the Emperor Charles v. Catherine's only brother, Juan, married Margaret of Austria, Emperor Maximilian's daughter, but he was to die in 1497 leaving no heir

OVERLEAF Joanna the Mad, the third daughter of Ferdinand and Isabella, and her husband, Philip the Fair, the eldest son of Maximilian and Mary of Burgundy. Portraits by Jean of Flanders. Philip and Joanna made an unexpected visit to England in 1506 and after her husband's death Henry VII explored the possibility of marrying the widowed Joanna himself.

Charles of Ghent, the
eldest son of Joanna and
Philip, later Emperor
Charles v. Through his
mother he inherited the
crown of Spain, and
through his father, the
Habsburg lands of Central
Europe, as well as the great
empire of the New World.
This drawing of Charles,
aged seven, was made
by Holbein.

behind him, a bitter blow to the schemes of Ferdinand and
Isabella. A Spanish bride for the infant Prince Arthur would
indubitably place the Tudors on a footing with the great House
of Habsburg.

In 1489 was concluded the Treaty of Medina del Campo,
signed near Valladolid for a marriage between Arthur and
Catherine. There was much haggling about the dowry, for
Henry demanded 200,000 crowns as well as jewels and a wardrobe befitting a great Princess. Ferdinand and Isabella were
quite plain: 'such a proceeding is against custom. Husbands
provide the dresses of their wives. They are willing to have as
many dresses and ornaments for the Princess Catherine as the
English may wish, provided the cost of them be deducted from
the marriage portion.' Ferdinand also pointed out that he had
four daughters to marry off and if all their prospective fathers-
in-law were as demanding as Henry, they would perforce have
to stay at home. As the Spanish envoy in London noted, though
Henry Tudor possessed 'many virtues, his love of money is too
great'; another Spaniard reported that he spent all the time he
was not in public 'in writing the accounts of his expenses in his
own hand'. He had invited the envoys to peep at the eighteen-
month-old Arthur while he was sleeping naked; they thought
him healthy enough, with qualities 'quite remarkable', yet the
formalities of ratifying the treaty proceeded slowly on both
sides. Many feared that betrothals of infants were solemnised
only in order to be broken when the political alliance they had
buttressed had outlived its usefulness. From time to time, discreet enquiries were made about Catherine's progress, and
suggestions made about her upbringing which would fit her
the more easily for life in England – for instance she should
become used to drinking wine, rather than water.

Ferdinand and Henry were each convinced that the other was
behaving in a devious manner; the one feared that Catherine
would become Queen of James IV of Scotland, the other that
Arthur would marry a Habsburg princess. At last a fresh marriage treaty was signed in October 1496, to be ratified a year
later, and the fact that this led to a proxy marriage owed much
to the Spanish ambassador in London, Dr Rodrigo de Puebla
who constantly stood by Henry. A shrewd diplomatist, de
Puebla was prominent in refurbishing the Anglo-Burgundian

88

alliance in 1496; in conjunction with de Ayala, the ambassador whom he had advised Ferdinand to send to James IV, he had helped in weaning the Scots from Warbeck's cause; and with de Ayala, too, he had been instrumental in bringing about the Anglo-Scottish truce. Above all, de Puebla emphasised to the Spanish sovereigns how secure was Henry's hold on his kingdom and underlined the advantages to them in having Catherine married to the heir of the House of Tudor. The ambassador even enticed Ferdinand by suggesting he could now 'dispose of England as though it belonged to Spain'. With the rebels defeated, the way was open for the next stage – a formal betrothal at Woodstock. A proxy marriage was then performed in London in the summer of 1498, after which Henry swore 'by his royal faith that he and the Queen were more satisfied with this marriage than with any other' in Christendom. Little Arthur had to endure a second proxy ceremony on Whitsun Day in 1499 in the chapel of the royal manor of Bewdley, where de Puebla again acted the part of proxy bride. The Prince took the arm of the deformed old man in his own and said in a clear voice that he rejoiced at the contract, in obedience to the Pope and to his father, and also for 'his deep and sincere love for the Princess, his wife'. The Bishop of Lincoln had felt uncomfortable at having to perform a secret ceremony, but de Puebla overcame his scruples and wrote to his sovereign that 'there is no longer any reason to fear fraud or cheating'. All England wanted Catherine to be wedded as soon as possible. Don Pedro de Ayala, the Spanish ambassador to Scotland, who now came to Westminster to reinforce Dr de Puebla – and intrigue against him – independently noted how much Henry desired the Princess's arrival, for this would elevate the King to the first rank of monarchs; he 'likes to be spoken much of and to be highly appreciated by the whole world'. Henry, he discovered, was unpopular, 'looking old for his years, but young for the sorrowful life he has lead'; yet Prince Arthur was 'much loved' by the people.

Catherine had been addressed as 'Princess of Wales' for as long as she could remember and had learned that she shared a common ancestor with Arthur in John of Gaunt, whose daughter Philippa (wife of King John of Portugal), was her maternal great-grandmother while another of his daughters –

Arthur, Prince of Wales, from a stained glass window in Malvern Priory.

Catherine – was also Catherine's maternal grandmother. It was not until the close of her fifteenth year that she finally left Spain, for besides the customary diplomatic delays there were sundry postponements of her sailing due in turn to a revolt of the Moors, illness and a gale. But eventually she bade farewell to her parents, received a last-minute codicil to Isabella's political testament for her, and after a rough passage landed at Plymouth early in October 1501. Reserved, but anxious to please, she was overwhelmed by the spontaneous welcome the West Country gave her. One of her train reported, 'She could not have been received with greater rejoicings if she had been the saviour of the world.' Catherine had, indeed, been long awaited. Escorted by the gentry, she rode by easy stages towards London, stopping at Exeter where the bells rang out, as they had rung when Warbeck was defeated, and here she was greeted in Henry's name by Lord Willoughby de Broke, Steward of the Royal Household. There still stands a timbered house at Charmouth, in Dorset, where Catherine and her ladies spent a night. It should have been Dr de Puebla, the architect of the marriage treaty who rode with her, but this honour had gone to Don Pedro, an aristocrat and a bishop. (Henry subsequently offered the little doctor a deanery and when he declined the preferment, the King assumed this must be because he wanted to marry and so he offered him a marriage portion.)

By the time Catherine reached Amesbury, near Stonehenge, she was welcomed by the Lord Treasurer, Thomas Howard, Earl of Surrey, and his Countess. After two more nights, her party was expected to reach the manor of Dogmersfield, the Bishop of Bath's country house near Basingstoke, and by then King Henry could restrain his curiosity no longer. He had intended meeting the Princess at Lambeth, but now he set out from Richmond with his son Arthur and a great entourage. When the Archbishop of Santiago and Doña Elvira Manuel, the Princess's chief lady-in-waiting, heard of the King's approach they decided that the requirements of Spanish etiquette must be rigidly followed; neither the bridegroom nor his father must set eyes on the girl until the wedding service, despite the series of betrothals and proxy marriages, so they sent off de Ayala to warn them away. Henry had not ridden so far to be snubbed in this way and without leaving his saddle called to those courtiers nearest him, 'my Lords, a council'. They unanimously resolved that as Catherine was already one of Henry's subjects he could not be restrained by Spanish custom. When they reached Dogmersfield he was told that Catherine was resting and he feared that he might be the victim of some wretched trick. Suppose the Princess were not, after all, the graceful young beauty men had alleged, but a plain child, ugly even, or deformed, whom Ferdinand and Isabella were attempting to have yoked to his Arthur, the Hope of England? 'Tell the Lords of Spain', Henry retorted firmly, 'that the King will see the Princess, even were she in bed.' He entered her dressing room and saw her face without a veil, and he smiled with satisfaction. She would do very well, very well indeed. He saw a girl with fine, expressive eyes and graceful features set off by long, light-brown hair: her lips seemed naturally to form a smile, and she moved her limbs daintily. In a year or so, this child would undoubtedly grow into a remarkably pretty young woman. Unable to speak to her in her own tongue and forgetting his Latin in the excitement, Henry merely nodded his approval and Catherine made a dignified curtsey. Within the hour Arthur, too, made his more formal entrance and the young couple who had exchanged love letters in a dead language almost as soon as each could hold a pen, eyed each other coyly. After dinner at the Bishop's expense, there was dancing into the winter evening. Henry could honestly write to the girl's parents that he 'much admired her beauty as well as her agreeable and dignified manner', while Arthur dutifully told them that he had never felt so much joy as when he first saw her sweet face, for 'no woman in the world could be more agreeable to him'. The bridegroom was a slim, fair-haired lad, overtall for his years, and pale. He was too much of a stripling to take part in the jousts or to make his mark in the butts. For all his princely bearing, Arthur had not, on close examination, the kind of physique that was expected from the reports of the Spaniards – who long ago had seen him as a baby, brimming with health in his cradle.

After a State entry into the City, they were married in St Paul's, when it fell to Henry, Duke of York, now ten and intended by his father for the celibate life of an archbishop, to give Catherine his hand as she walked down the aisle to the altar steps. The feasting, jousts and masques marking the wedding lasted for nearly a month, and then it was time for the Prince and Princess of Wales to set out for the Principality, which they would govern from Ludlow Castle. Here they were paid homage by the magnates and gentry of Wales, from Sir Rhys ap Thomas downwards, while from Richmond Henry VII began a fresh round of haggling with the ambassadors about Catherine's plate and jewels and the second half of her dowry.

During March there was an epidemic in Ludlow, perhaps a

bout of influenza rather than the sweating sickness, and Catherine was the first to feel unwell. Then Arthur became feverishly ill and was soon *in extremis*; after five months of marriage he was dead – 'of a consumption', it was said. A courier hastened towards London with the dreadful news which was broken to Henry by his confessor. He sent for Elizabeth of York and told her that they would 'take the painful sorrow together', for under the burden of this great grief he needed her support more than ever before. If, as the Spanish had averred,

Ode by the Welsh bard Rhys Nanmor, on the death of Arthur, Prince of Wales, in April 1502.

ABOVE Portrait of
Sir Thomas More as a
young man.

RIGHT Miniature of John Colet,
Dean of St Paul's, from an illuminated
manuscript of 1509.

94

E. Historics t̄ilu D. Ioh̄is Colenī Decani S. Pauli

On St George's Day, 1502, Prince
Arthur's body was removed from
Ludlow Castle to Worcester
Cathedral amid great pomp.
Henry had built a chantry chapel
for his son on the south side of the
high altar. This has open traceried
sides with niches containing
mourners. Above the tomb
is a flat ceiling with the
arms of England supported
by antelopes.

the coming of Catherine had been hastened by Warwick's death, retribution was seen in her ill-fated union with Arthur, which became infected (as Bacon put it) by 'a kind of malediction'.

Even though Warwick had been killed off, Henry *still* felt insecure, for Edmund de la Pole, Earl of Suffolk, the brother of Lincoln, had been persuaded to pick up the gauntlet of the White Rose. Henry had clipped his wings by forcing him to forego the rank of duke when he reached his majority in 1493 and by retaining much of the de la Pole inheritance in his own hands, yet Edmund seemed to be well favoured and had been active against the Cornish rebels. Towards the end of 1498 he killed a man in a fit of fury and, though he was pardoned, he resented the fact that he, a prince of the blood royal, should have to stand to a common law indictment for manslaughter. Next summer he fled abroad, staying with Sir James Tyrell at Guisnes Castle, and his flight alarmed King Henry. Sir Richard Guildford and others were required to induce him to return, on his allegiance, and if persuasion were of no avail to seize him. Suffolk came home voluntarily, but his feeling of insecurity increased with Warwick's death. Though he accompanied the King to Calais for his discussions with the Archduke Philip in 1500, there was great unease. Henry suspected that he was putting out feelers to the imperial court and he was said to be on close terms with Sir George Neville, Sir Robert Curzon and other Yorkists in exile. Rumour had it that the Emperor would lend Suffolk five thousand men. As Catherine of Aragon was leaving Spain, the Earl fled a second time, to join Maximilian, convinced that he must play his part as the legatee of the Yorkist party. A week before Arthur's marriage, he, together with Sir James Tyrell, his brother Lord William de la Pole, and Lord William Courtenay, the Earl of Devon's son, were proclaimed as traitors. Tyrell was seized and executed, while the young Lords Courtenay and de la Pole were imprisoned for the rest of Henry's reign. The King was taking no further chances. Anxious to lay his hands on Suffolk, he offered to pay Maximilian a subsidy if he would expel all English rebels from his dominions. Not for another four years would Henry have the Earl safely in the Tower, after a most fortunate turn of events.

4
King
and Court
1485-1509

Had we only the evidence of Michel Sittow's portrait of Henry, painted in 1505 (see p. 205), showing a rather mean face with thin lips, heavy eyes and a pointed nose, we might conclude that the King was an unattractive character, weighed down by the worries of keeping his throne and balancing his accounts. That portrait shows very forcefully one side of Henry, but there were other facets of his character – redeeming features indeed – which the artist chose not to depict, such as the serenity of a man firm in his faith, which Torrigiano's effigy brings out, and the gaiety and cheerfulness to which Bishop Fisher and others testify. Only a man with a real sense of humour would have put Lambert Simnel to work in his kitchens.

In an age in which the moral laxity of royal courts and the papal curia was a byword, Henry remained faithful to his wife. He had not embarked on a love match, but he came to show great tenderness towards Elizabeth, consoling her in a most moving way when Arthur died. Erasmus thought him an affectionate father. When Elizabeth of York died, the King seemed for a while almost overcome with natural grief and 'privily departed to a solitary place and would no man should resort unto him'. He was a pious man, regular in his devotions, often attending three Masses a day, and at times seemed more troubled by his own spiritual welfare than about his crown. For a King who had a reputation for miserliness, Henry was remarkably generous in his almsgiving, to sick and needy folk as well as to the Church.

There were three chief characteristics of Henry's Court which stemmed from the personality of its monarch. Though no scholar himself, he was not his mother's son for nothing, and was concerned to patronise learning, so that his courtiers included poets and historians of stature, and he was the first English sovereign to build a palace with a specification for a library. Second, he had an abiding love of music which, as likely as not, was inherited from his Welsh father. Last, and most significant, he developed the pageantry of the palace, elevating his kingship and endowing it with a mystique of its own.

There was nothing skimped or makeshift about the splendour of Henry's Court, which impressed foreigners by its dignity, its magnificence even. Louis XI, the 'Spider King' of France, had

PREVIOUS PAGES
A liveried groom holding a horse. This illustration is taken from the great Westminster Tournament Roll, produced for Henry VIII in 1511, but it portrays the style of dress worn by servants in the early sixteenth century. The groom is wearing a party-coloured gown, which represents the livery colours of his master.

RIGHT Torrigiano's terracotta bust of Henry VII.

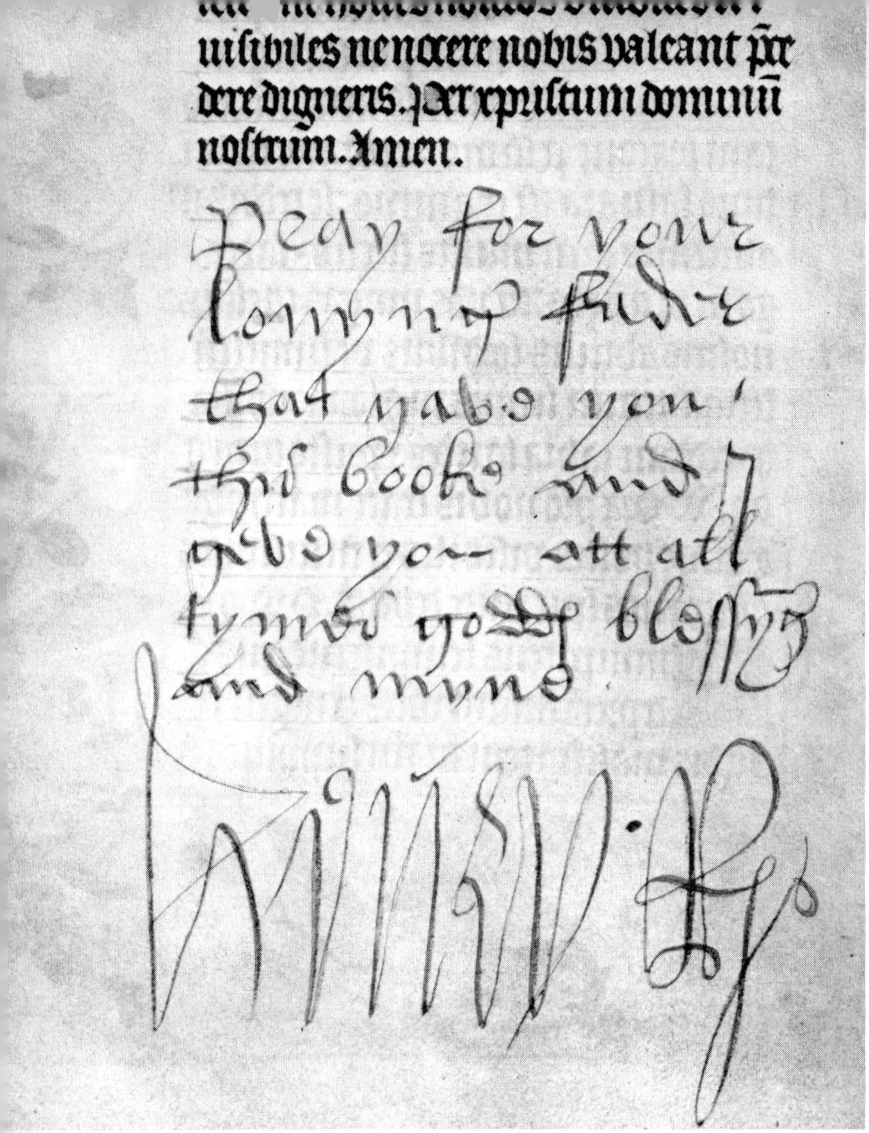

uisibiles ne nocere nobis valeant pre
dere digneris. Per xpm̃ dom̃nm̃
noftrum. Amen.

Pray for your
lovyng fader
that gave you
this booke and
geve you att all
tymes goddis blessyng
and myne

Henry R̄

Part of Henry VII's prayerbook, showing the prayer he added in his own writing for his daughter Margaret.

been content to wear shabby clothes and an old felt hat, but Henry Tudor reckoned that a King needed to appear in rich robes to command respect at home and abroad, and he spent more than he cared to remember on cloth-of-gold and of-silver, furs and silks as well as jewellery, for himself and his principal courtiers. Palace etiquette had been refined by Edward IV, who had modelled many secular ceremonies on Burgundian practice, and Henry was concerned to aim at high standards, whether it was in a procession to the chapel, the reception of an ambassador, or the ordering of a State banquet. Such pageantry was a most necessary prop to the throne. Henry instituted a bodyguard of Gentlemen Pensioners in their red livery, with

The well-dressed
courtier, from Jacob
Wimpfeling's *Adolescentia*,
printed in Strasbourg
by Martin Flach in 1500.

Colla fublimes hodie fuperba
Tollis in cœlos fubiturus atrum
Cras mifer læthum gelidis parata
Vermibus efca

flattened black caps, bearing halberds, modelled on the hand-
picked *corps* in the French King's household; after half a mil-
lenium, their lineal descendants are still on duty at the Tower of
London. In contrast to the Gentlemen Pensioners there were
the grooms, pages and other household staff in the Tudor livery
of white and green, with Henry's monogram. Processions, the
shouting of loyal *vivats*, the baring of heads and genuflexions in
the royal presence made everyday life at Court seem a heraldic
picture in motion.

Riding through Canterbury one day, Henry came across
some children singing out-of-doors and was so delighted with
what he heard that he gave them forty pence – the equivalent of

103

a carpenter's weekly wages. That incident illustrates not only a spontaneous generosity and a delight in the young, but also his love of music. He had a Welshman's appreciation of melody and, though no instrumentalist himself, he supported a body of musicians at Court, in addition to the chapel choir, which did rather more than provide fanfares and a martial beat for State occasions. From the King's household accounts, we can note purchases of organs and clavichords, and the sums he gave men such as William Cornish who wrote songs for him to sing. The Fleming Tinctoris, compiler of the first dictionary of music in these years, placed England well ahead of other countries. It was in this atmosphere that the future Henry VIII grew up, and his father must have been delighted by the boy's promise, for he approached professional standards in singing, playing and composition in his later 'teens.

Apart from visiting the provincial castles, like Winchester and Nottingham, and the small royal manor-houses in the shires, Henry made regular use of three residences in the capital and five in the Home Counties. The oldest was Westminster Palace, next to the Abbey that he would extend, sprawling over an extensive riverside site. Though Parliament and the law courts had made heavy inroads on available accommodation, this was both Henry's chief London house and the normal

Greenwich Palace, from an engraving by Basire. Henry refaced with red brick Margaret of Anjou's palace of 'Placentia' and renamed it Greenwich. It was to be one of the favourite palaces of the Tudors, and Henry VIII was born there.

setting for receptions and banquets. Here the King slept in Henry III's Painted Chamber, a vast dormitory, magnificent but chilly, like so much of Westminster Palace. The royal quarters on the upper floor of the White Tower in the Tower of London were cold and cramped and their associations were not of the happiest. Another stronghold, Baynard's Castle in Thames Street, became transformed during the reign into a comfortable family town house, so that it was 'far more beautiful and commodious' than a citadel.

Greenwich was a relatively recent acquisition of the Crown. A splendid mansion had been built there in a park by the Regent Humphrey, Duke of Gloucester, who called it 'Bella Court'. On his death it had been occupied by Margaret of Anjou, who inserted a great many windows, covered the floor with terra-cotta tiles and ornamented the outside with pillars bearing her heraldic emblem, the marguerite. To underline her ownership, Queen Margaret had changed the name to 'Placentia', or 'Pleasaunce'. Now another Lancastrian was in residence and, symbolically, the name was again changed – to Greenwich. Henry VII was fond of the palace and refaced the building with red brick. His mother proved a rich benefactress of the Franciscan convent just outside the walls, and here her second grandson, whose accession she would live to witness, was born.

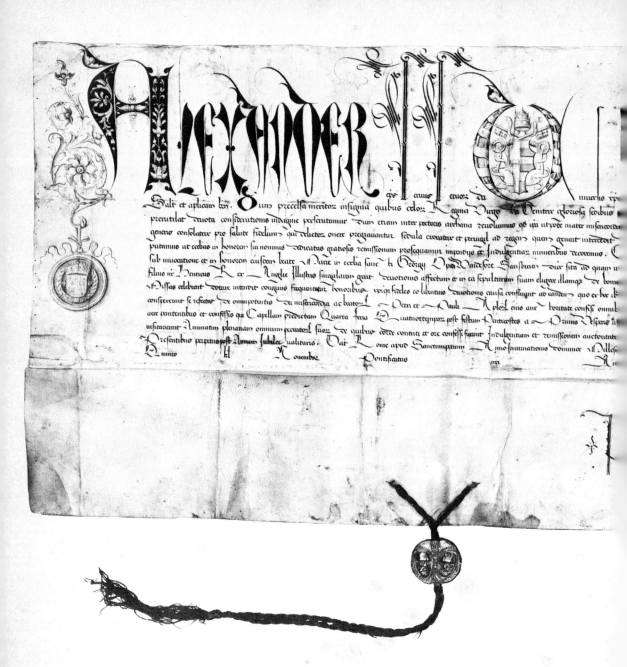

ABOVE Papal indulgence
from Alexander VI, to all
visitors to the Chapel of
St Mary which Henry VII
planned to endow at
St George's Chapel
Windsor.

RIGHT Richmond Palace,
as drawn by Anthony van
Wyngaerde in 1555.
Henry's great palace, with
its lofty towers and
complex bay windows,
stands in the centre of the

illustration. To the right of
the palace lies part of the
former palace of Sheen,
which was burnt out at
Christmas 1498. This was
probably the great hall or
chapel, left to stand in ruins.

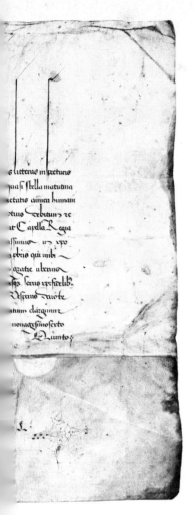

Not five miles away was Eltham, in Kent, with its moat and great hall, redolent of Plantagenet England; too small a house for an enlarged Court, it was ideal for a retreat in good hunting country. Of Windsor little need be said: Henry was committed to completing the great St George's Chapel, which Edward IV had begun, though he would not live to see its consecration. Certainly the noisy activities of workmen on the site shattered the peace of Castle Green and Henry rarely held the annual chapter of the Order of the Garter at Windsor. The palace furthest from London in regular use was Woodstock in Oxfordshire, in the grounds of what three centuries later became Marlborough's Blenheim; ancient Woodstock was smaller even than Eltham and rather decayed.

The last royal residence was Sheen in Surrey, called after the Old English word for a beauty spot, and soon to be renamed. Henry had planned to keep Christmas at Sheen in 1498 but on the night of 21 December, while the royal family was in residence, fire broke out. The place was gutted. Much valuable furniture, jewels and plate was destroyed – the New Year's gifts for the royal children probably went up in smoke like everything else; but no lives were lost. The King decided to replace the ruined manor-house with a magnificent residence in the Gothic style, to be built, like a college, round a paved court. Within two years the new palace was ready for occupation. Henry has a reputation for carefulness in money matters but at Sheen nothing was skimped; there was lead in plenty on the roof, and the number of windows must have made

contemporaries regard the building as a crystal palace. The royal quarters, the Privy Lodging, were decorated with fourteen turrets; and the chapel, unlike any parish church of the time, had pews – 'handsome cathedral seats' in fact. But the chief feature was the tower; and those privileged to climb the one hundred and twenty steps had a wonderful view of the country from its top.

To crown his achievement Henry VII, in the manner of a dictator, gave the palace a new name. At the time of Bosworth he had been Earl of Richmond, the Yorkshire honour, but with his accession this title had merged in the Crown. He now perpetuated the name by decreeing that what had previously been termed Sheen should from henceforth be Richmond Palace.

And yet – 'all his goodly houses, so richly decked and apparelled, his walls and galleries of royal pleasure, his gardens large and wide with knots curiously wrought, his orchards set with vines and trees most delicious, his marvellous richness and treasure, his meats and drinks, were they never so diligently prepared' became a pain and reproach to him. It was almost, thought Bishop Fisher, as if King Henry realised his kingdom was not of this world – and such, perhaps, was the dearest wish of his mother in her last years.

Though Lady Margaret, Countess of Richmond and Derby, was seldom at her son's Court after her last husband's death, preferring to live at Woking, her influence was pervasive in intellectual and spiritual life. She was renowned for her faith no less than for her good works. She would begin her strict sequence of devotions at five every morning and though she suffered from rheumatism which often reduced her to tears, this never stopped her from spending long periods on her knees in prayer. Next to her skin she wore a hair shirt and in place of regal fineries she wore modest robes, much like a nun's habit. She was happiest reading and translating devotional works, such as *The Imitation of Christ*. Margaret maintained twelve aged paupers in her house at Woking, herself serving them with meals when they were ill and comforting them as they approached death. Since her only child from her four marriages had become King, she had no family calls on her fortune and, spending remarkably little on herself, she used her wealth for educational and other charitable purposes.

In 1497 Margaret chose as her confessor John Fisher from Beverley, who had graduated somewhat later than most of the men attending the schools at Cambridge, but had in quick succession become senior proctor and master of his college, Michaelhouse. Lady Margaret soon realised the worth of the man – his learning, his forcefulness of character, his integrity and his endearing humility. In the earliest years of the new century he became Vice-Chancellor of the University, then Chancellor, Bishop of Rochester, the first Professor of Divinity of his patron's foundation and President of Queen's College, a post made available to him so that he could the more readily supervise at Margaret's behest the transformation of God's House into Christ's College, which she had so richly endowed. What influenced men most was Fisher's pulpit oratory, rather than his reformist zeal. Henry, who was going on pilgrimage to the shrine of Our Lady of Walsingham, accompanied his mother to Cambridge in 1506 to see the progress being made on the buildings of the Lancastrian foundation of King's College, of which the chapel still lacked a roof. Erasmus was in the royal party and his hand can be detected in the statutes for Christ's College. Right at the end of her life, the Lady Margaret was using Fisher's aid to found another collegiate society, St John's, destined, like Corpus Christi at Oxford, erected by his friend Richard Fox, to become a cradle of the New Learning.

William Caxton had already turned fifty when he opened his printing press in the almonry of Westminster Abbey in 1476. Despite close connexions with the Court, changes of dynasty affected him little and he found the Tudors no less discerning patrons than the Yorkists. Henry VII asked him to print the *Feats of Arms*, he dedicated his *Eneydos* to Prince Arthur, and there was constant encouragement from the Countess of Richmond for all that he undertook. Like all great publishers, he balanced the formation of public taste with a careful study of the market for his wares, so that most of his books achieved several impressions. Chaucer's *Canterbury Tales*, Mallory's *Morte d'Arthur* and other chivalric romances were among his best-sellers and there was always a ready market for devotional works and English versions of Latin authors, which he translated himself. In this age of degree, Caxton made a point of catering for different kinds of readers. Not every book, he said,

OPPOSITE Lady Margaret Beaufort, Countess of Richmond, Henry VII's devout and rather awesome mother. Portrait by an unknown artist.

110

Mary Countess of Richmond

SQWENT ME SQWIENT.

was 'convenient for every rude and simple man', not every volume was fit for ladies to peruse and some of his products were specifically for 'clerks and gentlemen that understand gentleness and science'. Then there were schoolbooks, like *Caton*, full of homely proverbs, which he thought 'the best book to be taught to young children in school' and his *Knight of the Tower* which he translated for his daughters – moral tales, spiced with an everyday coarseness, that he reckoned were essential reading for a 'gentlewoman, of whatever estate she be'. A remarkable production was *The Book of Good Manners*, a collection of scriptural texts and glosses to remind the lower orders not to behave like brute beasts.

Caxton's prolific output as translator and printer spread knowledge, narrowed the gulf between clergy and laity and began the standardisation of English grammar and vocabulary. On the day he died in 1491, he was translating another Latin text for the press. His German assistant, Wynkyn de Worde, carried on the business in Westminster using his fount, and frequently sought the advice of the Lady Margaret.

One of Pynson's books that reached a wide public was the English version of *The Ship of Fools* (1509), by the Black monk Alexander Barclay, who enjoyed Margaret Beaufort's patronage. This was rather more than a verse translation of the German Brandt's work, for Barclay's ship carried a native crew, courtiers and merchants. 'My speech is rude and my terms common and rural', wrote the monk in his foreword and, as a result, this satire of clergy and laymen adrift in perilous seas with Folly at the helm achieved enormous and continuing popularity. The success of Caxton, de Worde and Richard Pynson (who specialised in law books) prompted the founding by John Tate, son of a Lord Mayor of London, of the first paper mill in England, at the county town of Hertford in 1496.

One of the Grooms of the King's Chamber was Stephen Hawes, who reckoned himself the only true poet left in England. Like Lydgate, whom he took as his master, he came from Suffolk but though after graduating at Oxford he had travelled abroad, he remained insular in outlook and, even more, looked to the past for inspiration, embroidering with rich allegory the theme of knightly chivalry which had been the stock in trade of romantic verse for three centuries. He saw

John Fisher, Bishop of Rochester, who was Lady Margaret's confessor. On Lady Margaret's instruction he founded first Christ's College and then St John's College, Cambridge. This drawing of Fisher was made in the 1530s by Holbein.

Caxton under the Tudors

In 1476 Caxton set up his press in the almonry at Westminster Abbey.
He was patronised first by Edward IV and his Court, and then by
Henry VII and his mother, Lady Margaret Beaufort. He printed the
Feats of Arms for Henry, and dedicated *Eneydos* to Prince Arthur.
His output was enormous, for not only did he print over ninety-six
separate works and editions, but also undertook the translations of
many of the books himself.

ABOVE Caxton's device,
consisting of his initials and
trade mark. He used this device
in eleven of his books and
broadsheets.

LEFT A page from Caxton's
Mirrour of the World which he
printed in 1481. This is the first
of his books to contain
woodcut illustrations.

ABOVE Woodcut of a
printing press,
dating from *c.* 1500.

Here foloweth the thyrde boke of that noble prynce kyng Arthur.

¶ How kyng Arthur toke a wyf and wedded Gueneuer doughter to Leodegraūce kyng of the londe of Camelyarde with whome he had the Rounde table. Capl'm prīmū.

IN the begynnynge of Arthur after ꝑ he was chosen kyng by aduenture ⁊ by grace for the moost parte of the barons knewe not that he was Vtherpendragons sone. But as Merlyn made

it openly knowen. But yet many kynges ⁊ lordes helde grete warre ayenst hym for ꝑ cause / but well Arthur ouer came them all / for the moost parte the dayes of his lyf he was ruled moche by the counseyll of Merlyn. So it fell on a tyme ꝑ kyng Arthur sayd vnto Merlyn / my barons wyll lete me haue no rest but nedes I must take a wyf / ⁊ I wyll none take but by thy coūseyl ⁊ by thyne aduyse / it is well done sayd Merlyn that ye take a wyf / for a man of your boūte ⁊ noblesse sholde not be without a wyf. Now is ther ony that ye loue more than an other. Ye sayd kyng Arthur. I loue Gueneuer the kynges doughter Leodegraūce of the londe of Camelyarde / the whiche holdeth in his house the table roūde that

d iiij

LEFT Wynkyn de Worde's
version of Mallory's great
romance, *Morte d'Arthur*,
printed in Westminster in
1498. The woodcut shows
the marriage of Arthur
and Guinivere.

ABOVE Dürer's engraving of the
Ship of Fools for Sebastian Brandt.
This was translated into English
by the Black monk Alexander
Barclay in 1509 and printed by
Richard Pynson.

Stephen Hawes, one of Henry VII's Grooms of the Chamber, created courtly verses imbued with themes of medieval romance and chivalry. This woodcut is taken from his *Examples of Virtues*, printed for Hawes by Wynkyn de Worde in 1510. The narrator, accompanied by 'Discretion' meets a 'lady olde and amyable, Sittynge in a castell both fressh and gay, on an olyphaintes back in strength so stable'.

as his mission the writing of 'books of moral virtue', like *The Conversation of Swearers*; reading between its somewhat turgid lines it would seem that manners at Court had deteriorated since the death of Elizabeth of York. Hawes's *tour de force* was *Pastime of Pleasure, or the History of Grand Amour and La Bel Pucell*, printed by Wynkyn de Worde. The courtly verses extend to five thousand eight hundred lines in forty-five chapters, telling the allegorical tale of Grand Amour's wooing of La Bel Pucell. Having mastered the seven liberal arts and imbibed the teaching of the Lady Grammar, our hero first encounters his lady love in the garden by the Tower of Music and offers her his heart. Her parents have her whisked away to foreign parts, leaving her lover to study geometry and astronomy before an attachment at the Tower of Chivalry, to be trained by Minerva. After winning the sword of honour he sets out on his quest for his beloved – a pilgrimage which involves outwitting a dwarf, who mocks women's modesty, slaying a giant with three heads, representing the world, the flesh and the devil, and killing another monster embodying the seven deadly sins. His efforts win the approval both of the Lady Perseverance and of Venus, who intercedes with his sweetheart, yet he has still to cross a barren desert before at last he sees the towers of her palace, built on an inaccessible island. Grand Amour's strength is failing, yet he has enough spirit to outwit an armour-plated monster, Privy Malice, and finally reaches La Bel Pucell. The tale does not end with their marriage, for Master Hawes introduces fresh hazards in the characters of Old Age, Avarice and Policy, so that it is not until his deathbed that the great lover's soul is saved.

For all the limitations of the versifying, this romance was very popular with Henry's courtiers. Hawes opened magic casements onto a characteristic fairyland, peopled by knights-at-arms, beautiful damsels in need of protection, giants and demons who had to be overcome and fabulous birds whose song turned the prosaic world of Henry's Court into an enchanted garden. Though in the medieval tradition, the *Pastime of Pleasure* had one novel element, as its full sub-title makes plain – '... containing the knowledge of the seven sciences and the course of man's life', Stephen Hawes successfully convinces the reader that learning is an essential quality of a gentleman. This poem announces the theme to be elaborated by Baldassare Castiglione in his *Il Cortigiano*, which became the manual of courtiers' behaviour throughout Western Europe; and it is tempting to think that when Castiglione came to Henry's Court in 1503 to stand proxy for his master Guy, Duke of Urbino, at his installation as a Knight of the Garter, he talked with Hawes about the qualities of Grand Amour. In another of the poems, *The Example of Virtue*, he interrupts a series of regular seven-line stanzas with a surprisingly modern passage:

> See
> Ye
> Be
>   Kind
> Again.
> My pain
> Retain
>   In Mind

which is followed by a gradual increase of the metre to lines of six syllables and then a gradual contraction to one again. Such experimentation in metre and 'shaped' verses is not what one would have expected from a Groom of the Chamber.

Among the learned men at Court was Bernard André, a blind Augustinian friar from Toulouse, who had already earned a reputation for Latin verse composition. André had been introduced to Henry by Bishop Fox, whom he continued to regard as his Maecenas, and within a few years of Bosworth had been appointed Poet Laureate. Later he also held the office of historiographer-royal and, becoming a secular priest, received various benefices. The Frenchman even taught at Oxford, for Henry's grant of a pension mentions 'the increase of virtue and learning coming to many persons at Oxford and elsewhere from his teaching'. As a result he was chosen as principal tutor for Prince Arthur until the latter's marriage.

In his role of Laureate André produced a series of panegyrics on Henry Tudor and his family. If Erasmus rated his literary performance as indifferent it may not have been an impartial judgment, for the two had quarrelled about the tardy repayment of a loan André had made to Erasmus. It is hard to imagine that a blind man served, as some have said, as Keeper of the King's library, a fine collection of manuscripts and books that foreign envoys thought was one of the sights of London; the first royal librarian was in fact a cleric from Lille named Quintin Paule. About the turn of the century, André began writing a laudatory life of the King, but he did not reach much later than the *annus mirabilis* of 1497. Soon he had left Court, to live out his days as rector of Guisnes near Calais, an appropriate niche for a Frenchman. To ensure the continued payment of his stipend, he promised Henry that he would present him with a new literary composition every year. One such was his poem in French on the theme of the Twelve Trials of his master.

From 1501 Polydore Vergil, a scholar from Urbino, resided in England, to which he had come as sub-collector of Peter's Pence. Once Henry was satisfied that the ageing André would never produce a sustained historical narrative, he invited the Italian to write a history of England from the earliest times down to his own reign. Trained in Italy in the critical ways of Renaissance scholarship, Polydore approached the British past without preconceived ideas, and his book was to prove a milestone in historical studies. He broke away from the methods of the monastic chroniclers and civic annalists who had taken at their face value earlier writings and perpetuated past myths about Brutus, Arthur and divine intervention. Moreover, he could write a telling narrative and his story was the more fascinating for being as near the truth as he could make it. Of course, once his work was published, in 1535, certain Englishmen were dismayed that a foreigner should have dared to dismiss old patriotic myths, but his first royal patron recognised Polydore's worth and could guide him with personal information when he arrived at his days in exile and the early years of his reign, much as a statesman of today writes his memoirs. The man who had begun his career as chamberlain to Pope Alexander VI now became a prebendary of Hereford Cathedral and Archdeacon of Wells. The first 'modern' historian of England was anything but a dull dog.

A far greater poet, and an Englishman, was to succeed André as Laureate – John Skelton. He was the first man under royal patronage to write English verse. One of his earliest compositions had been an elegy on the death of Edward IV, but he soon turned his talents to the Lancastrians and, after earning the praise and patronage of the Lady Margaret, entered Henry's employ in 1488. Early years at Cambridge, followed by the study of rhetoric at Oxford, singled him out for an educational post and when the future Henry VIII was seven Skelton was appointed his tutor. He later claimed to have taught the Prince to write and to have introduced him to the Muses. Since it was two and a half centuries before orthography hardened there was no irony in the poet's lines:

> The honor of England I lernyd to spelle
> In dyngnyte roialle that doth excelle.

For his young charge Skelton wrote *Speculum Principis*, a treatise on how royalty should behave. He was present at Eltham Palace in 1499 when Thomas More and Lord Mountjoy introduced Erasmus to the English Court. King Henry VII and Prince Arthur were away for the day and in their absence the nine-year-old Prince Henry acted as host. Little Prince Edmund was in his nurse's arms and Mary, the future Queen of France,

OPPOSITE 'What can it avail', a poem by John Skelton, Poet Laureate to the early Tudors, which was 'an invective against clergy of all sorts and degrees'.

was playing on the rushes on the floor. More, knowing the custom of the royal nursery, had brought with him a nicely-penned Latin verse, but Erasmus was empty-handed and rather annoyed that he had not been fore-warned. During dinner young Henry sent the scholar a note inviting something from his pen and back in his lodging at Richmond Erasmus wrote an ode praising Henry VII, his children and his realm, which, a year later was printed with the collection of *Adages*, a volume that went through sixty editions in his lifetime. Erasmus had been struck not only by the scholar Prince's poise and learning but by Master Skelton's outstanding ability; he was, he wrote, 'a light and ornament of British literature'.

But Skelton was no sycophant, like Bernard André. In an age when poets generally praised their patrons, he spoke his un-fettered opinions, mocking lofty peers and staid ecclesiastics, and even daring to tackle political themes. He certainly had contempt of convention and made plain the insincerities of the courtier's life, as we can appreciate from his satirical *Bouche of Court* – the technical term for the right to free rations at the King's expense which was so blatantly abused. King Henry applauded the man's frankness, no less than his poetic gifts, and gave him a dress of white and green, on which was embroidered in silken letters of gold the word 'Calliope', the name of the ancient Muse of epic poetry. Cambridge University even gave Skelton the privilege of wearing this dress in place of full academic robes. Soon Skelton took to spending longer away from Court at his Norfolk rectory and won a wider fame with his burlesque *Book of Philip Sparrow*, perhaps the original of the nursery rhyme *Who Killed Cock Robin?* His life was as unortho-dox as his verse, for when the Bishop of Norwich ordered him to put away his mistress, he ejected her by the front door only to help her return by a window, and then had the impudence to show off their son to the parishioners of Diss from the pulpit. His principal works were to be written in the next reign.

Though not often at Court herself in these years, the Lady Margaret's influence was pervasive in every branch of scholar-ship. But above all others there was the King, studious rather than learned, pragmatic in his approach, teaching by example his successor in statecraft. 'Certainly', wrote a Spaniard, 'there could be no better school in the world than the society of such

quis [con]surget [mihi] adversus malignantes aut quis
stabit mecum adversus operantes iniquitatem /
nomine domini

what can hyt avayle
to dryve forthe a snayle
or to make a sayle
of an herynge tayle
to ryme or to rayle
to wryte or to endyte
eyther for to delyte
... or ... for to despyte
... ... to dyspyse
... dyd mad of ... ...
nyce to ...
... ... for to spyle
to teche or to preche
no reason wold rehers
... say thus or say that
... ... ys ... fatte
... ... he wott not whate
nor whereof he speketh
he preteth he preketh
... ... he ...
the ... he thrid
he pryteth he payzd
he ... he ...
he ... he smateth
he ... he ...
... he speke playne
... he lacketh brayne
... ... hurt a foole
... ... to stole

... ... stole
... ... sytte
for ... ... wryte
... ... he grete
... ... on the hed
hyt stondyth in no sted
the ... they ... ...
hyt may ... well be
or els they wold see
... ...
... worldly ...
... ...
... ...

And fykyll falsenes
... ...
to ...
And yf they stonde in dovte
who brought y ... abovte
... name ye John ...
And purpose to ... ...
all my ... ...
lyke a clarke ...
for thou me ... ...
... ...
... rayne ...
... ... styd ...
And yf thou take well ... wythe
hyt hathe in hyt ... ...
for as for ... ...
hyt ys wronge ... ...
for the ...
... ...
the ... ...
... ... complayne
vppon the ... ...
they ... ...
... ...
Alas they make me ...
for ... ...
the thinge ys put in ...
the play ... ...
they ... ...
... thou ...
Above the ... ...
... men ... ...
how they ... none ...
... ... shepe ...
... ... away ...
... floke of wolle
... they love a lotte
of wolle amonge the flocke
And ... for y ...
a ... ... a ...
And make therof a hepe
they ... ... they ...
all to have ...
... ... all ...

a father' as Henry. 'He is so wise and attentive to everything; nothing escapes his attention.' Louis XI of France had always wanted to get his teeth into facts and despised opinions, but Henry Tudor knew by instinct that in politics a point of view could be no less significant than a hard fact.

'Frugal to excess in his own person', it was said of Henry, 'he does not change any of the ancient usages of England at his court, keeping a sumptuous table.' It was not uncommon for seven hundred people to dine at his expense at Westminster and on red-letter days the menu could extend to sixty separate dishes. With such open-handed liberality, it is not surprising that Ferdinand of Spain's agent, de Puebla, dined 'every day in the Palace' of choice, or that the outspoken Skelton should have lampooned those who exploited the system by bringing along their own servants and hangers-on for free meals. The system was not to be reformed until Cardinal Wolsey's prime.

Henry's subjects expected a King of England to live in style, not to behave as a Welsh petty chieftain. Magnificence in dress, though costly, was a sound investment and from his experience of the Courts of Brittany and France Henry could view the Court scene in a detached way. His consort did all that he expected of her in projecting the right image of herself and her ladies. When an ambassador had an audience of Elizabeth of York at an unexpected hour, he found her with thirty-two 'companions of angelical appearance, and all we saw there seemed very magnificent and in splendid style, as was suitable for the occasion'.

The Court entertainments which enlivened the long winter evenings had their place in government propaganda. On Twelfth Night 1494 King and Queen processed 'through both the Halls' at Westminster between the end of divine service and the start of a great banquet. The feast was followed by 'a play with a pageant of St George with a castle and twelve lords and twelve ladies disguised, which did dance'. It was a typically patriotic theme, slanted to enhance the crown and its wearer, and the novelty of the occasion was the disguising, a device introduced from Italy.

The climax of the entertainments devised at Court was the welcome to Princess Catherine of Aragon in November 1501. Henry wrote to Catherine's parents that 'great and cordial

Woodcut of a tower, resembling the set pieces composed by Master William Cornish for the revelries at Court. From an early sixteenth-century edition of Terence in French.

rejoicings have taken place'. Indeed, the festivities marking the royal wedding were in every sense brilliant, impressing all beholders, and in view of the great numbers of Londoners and others who watched the tournaments and eavesdropped at other events it was natural for the King to add that 'the whole people have taken part.' In the lists in front of Westminster Hall, a tree of chivalry was set up for the first time, on which the challengers hung their shields. More remarkable were the processions of the knights with their servants into the lists. William Courtenay entered concealed in a dragon, escorted by a giant; the Earl of Essex came in a pageant car resembling a green mountain, while others rode in a float decked out as a ship, with seamen firing cannon.

In the evenings there were banquets, followed by music, disguisings and dances, with pageant cars and set-pieces for stately revels on the themes of marriage, the honour of Spain and the glories of England, all rich in allegory. In one pageant, twelve lords were hidden in an arbor, while the twelve ladies with whom they would dance entered the hall in a transparent lantern. For light relief there was a Spanish acrobat. With these ambitious stage-settings devised by Master William Cornish, a gentleman of the Chapel Royal, the hall was transformed by candlelight into fairyland. One night the set piece was a tower, with lusty knights in the lower storey and coy maidens upstairs, and this tower was pulled into the hall by 'sea-horses', escorted by 'mermaids', inside each of which lurked a chorister 'singing right sweetly and with great harmony'. A further entertainment, more elaborate than the others, consisted of three scenes enacted round a castle, in which disguised ladies resided, a ship sailed by knights errant, who made a raid into the Castle of Love across a ladder, hopeful of wooing the virtuous inmates, and a mountain on which both sexes later disported before they clambered down to dance together. This particular 'disguising' which embraced singing, spoken dialogue, action and dancing, was the first masque proper in England. Cornish, the master of these revels, found little scope for his ingenuity during the last years of Henry's reign, but with a new monarch was to be given a free hand – and a considerable budget – for devising a spectacular series of productions.

The gaiety of Prince Arthur's wedding festivities was never recaptured in Henry VII's day. The Prince's sudden death, followed so closely by that of his mother, produced a sombre reaction. The Court remained dignified in Henry's last years, but the laughter and the merriment had vanished; there were no more disguisings, and tournaments and banquets were rare, for the King found nothing really worth celebrating. Instead he found diversion on a more modest level in the antics of the man who ate sea-coal and in the Flemish giantess. Chess or cards for stakes with the gentlemen of the Chamber passed the long evenings. It was not so surprising that a widower past his prime should be following a more staid routine, even though he tried to hunt whenever he could, for the chase remained the sport of kings.

5 Winds

ALIS

tartaria per totum

tartaria per totum

Hic domina cham maior tartaroru imperator [?]

Hic dñat presbiter johanes imperator [?] totius indic

SINVS GANGETIC

SINVS [?]

CEANVS
NDICVS
ERIDIONAL

of Change 1485-1509

PREVIOUS PAGES Map of 1490 from *Insularium Illustratum*, showing 'true modern form of Africa according to the description of the Portuguese', with notes on the African voyages made by Diego.

OPPOSITE Portrait of Vasco da Gama, the Portuguese explorer, who found the sea-routes to India in 1498, and became second viceroy of India in 1524.

BELOW Miniature of Henry the Navigator (1394–1400), the fourth son of John I of Portugal. Henry's expeditions discovered the Madeira Islands and much of the coast of West Africa.

M AN'S INTELLECTUAL HORIZONS were expanding, for the flowering of the Renaissance affected not merely art and letters but every aspect of human life. In scholarship the rediscovery of Greek had added a new dimension to classical studies and made possible fresh interpretations of the New Testament. A fearless search for truth and beauty, which the Humanist outlook embraced, questioned anew the whole purpose of man, and there was a restless urgency in all intellectual endeavour which would lead inevitably to disputes with authority, chiefly the authority of the Church. In England, as on the Continent, the topic of reforming the Church was freely discussed, yet despite undercurrents of anti-clerical feeling, few would have imagined that Europe was on the edge of an abyss and that within eight years of Henry's death Martin Luther would nail his Theses to the door of Wittenberg Palace Church as the first, dramatic step of a Protestant Reformation. In contrast, John Colet and the Oxford Reformers of Henry Tudor's reign were seeking for a renewal of Christian life which would reform the Church from within. Their influence was such that when, under Henry VIII, England broke with Rome, the shape of the new nationalist Church would owe very little to Luther and other Continental reformers.

The globe was shrinking as rapidly as man's knowledge of himself and his universe was expanding. In the year of the battle of Stoke the Portuguese Bartholomew Diaz, pioneering in the great tradition of Prince Henry the Navigator, rounded the Cape of Good Hope, although the gale which he encountered was so severe that his crew forced him to return to Lisbon. Five years later Columbus crossed the Atlantic, carrying a letter for the Great Khan of Cathay, convinced that he had found a western sea route to Asia. He made three further voyages to the New World, discovering the islands of Central America and the West Indies and establishing a Spanish colony on Hispaniola. It was not until 1501 that his successor, Amerigo Vespucci, in the service of the King of Portugal, convinced himself that the coast of Brazil was not an outlying segment of Asia but part of a new world, and the German map-maker Martin Waldseemüller was sufficiently satisfied with his explanation that he named the continent America after Vespucci. Before that date Vasco da Gama had sailed forth to

Dom Vasco da gama 16°

find the sea route to India, in the wake of Diaz, and in May 1498 reached Calicut on the Malabar Coast. England, on the extremity of Europe, made its contribution to the discoveries by Cabot's voyage to 'Newfoundland' under royal patronage though, as we shall see, fishermen from Bristol and other West Coast ports had already visited those waters in search of cod, rather than looking for a route to the spices and silks of the east.

For Henry, so unswervingly orthodox in his religious beliefs and practices, there was nothing suspect about the 'New Learning'; like his mother, he considered all knowledge to be a true handmaiden of religion, every discovery to be a further revelation of the divine purpose. In that age of intellectual ferment, with the revolutionary redrawing of maps, he remained unperturbed, at last secure in the authority of his kingship, unaware of the strength of the winds of change.

There had been significant cultural links between England and the Italian states earlier in the fifteenth century, but the most fruitful influence came as a result of the visit which Cornelio Vitelli paid to Oxford in the mid-1460s. Vitelli knew classical Greek and persuaded young William Grocyn of New College of its importance. Grocyn has been fairly described by Hallam as 'the patriarch of English learning', for he spanned the gap between medieval and modern scholarship. The first English Humanist proper, he gathered round him at Oxford such men as William Warham, destined to become Archbishop of Canterbury, William Lyly, the grammarian, Thomas Linacre, the physician, and John Colet, the preaching Dean and educationalist. Grocyn attracted them to explore with him the New Learning that stemmed from Italy and rediscovering of Greek texts.

Not until 1489, when Grocyn was a mature scholar of forty-three, did he pay his first visit to Italy, to drink at the fountain-head. By then Thomas Linacre was already well-established in Florence as a fellow pupil of Giovanni de' Medici, the future Pope Leo x, before migrating to Padua to study medicine. A prodigy at Greek, assisting in establishing the Aldine text of Aristotle, Linacre was persuaded by his reading of ancient writers to turn to science and was happiest when working on his edition of Galen. He continued to keep a foot in both camps, as a rounded, Renaissance man. On Linacre's qualifying as a

Thomas Linacre, a scholar and Henry VII's personal physician. A prodigy at classical Greek, he served as tutor to Prince Arthur and a generation later, supervised the education of Henry VIII's elder daughter, Mary. Linacre played a leading part in the foundation of the Royal College of Physicians.

doctor, Henry VII appointed him his physician and he attended Warham, Fox and leading courtiers, yet he also served as tutor to Prince Arthur and, a generation later, would supervise the education of Henry VIII's daughter, Princess Mary. More than any other man, Linacre was responsible for the foundation of the Royal College of Physicians. By his Will he endowed the two absorbing interests of his life – learning and physical medicine, for he left the front part of his London house in Knight Rider Street to the College of Physicians and the rear portion to Merton College, Oxford, and he also bequeathed money for a readership in medicine at Oxford. In recent years Oxford University has given his name its due by founding as a postgraduate society Linacre College whose membership bridges the two cultures.

Grocyn, Colet and their friends found Florence a stimulating place at the time when Savonarola was denouncing the corruption of Medici rule and demanding the assembly of a general council to set the Church in order and to cleanse the Augean stables of Rome. The English scholars certainly became infected during their stay with the importance of a religious revival and returned home convinced that Humanist studies and theology were indeed most compatible. Some of the great Italian artists of the Renaissance were proclaiming a very different creed, depicting the divine as human and the human as divine, while certain thinkers were already formulating a secular rationale. In England, however, the New Learning strengthened Christian doctrine and emphasised the need for reforming both the Church as an institution and individuals' lives by a new evangelism, such as the friars had preached in the thirteenth century. It was to be no accident that Englishmen would make their greatest contribution to scholarship in the next generation by revising texts and translations of the Scriptures.

On his return to Oxford, Grocyn gave the first public lectures in Greek, where his most promising pupil was a page in the household of Archbishop Morton, named Thomas More, whose patron had sent him to Canterbury Hall to further his studies. More's father came to think that the study of Greek was a subject of dangerous modernity for a boy of fourteen – an indication of how revolutionary the New Learning seemed to some – and set him on a career as a lawyer. By the turn of the century, Grocyn had settled in London to become the leading spirit in a group of lively minds. A man of European reputation, he was lauded by Erasmus as 'the patron and preceptor of us all'. There was still a twinkle about him, where Colet seemed puritanical and severe. No 'dry as dust' scholar, Grocyn had once written a charming Latin epigram on a young lady who had teased him; put into English it ran:

> A snowball white at me did Julia throw,
> Who would suppose it? Fire was in that snow.
> Julia alone can quench my hot desire
> But not with Snow, or Ice, but equal Fire.

The young Erasmus, visiting England for the first time in 1499, was amazed at the state of learning and the generosity of scholars. At dinner parties, he said, 'the good cheer would have satisfied Epicurus and the table-talk would have pleased Pythagoras.' To another friend, Erasmus praised the delights of England and the giants with whom he sat:

> I never liked anything so much before. I find the climate both pleasant and wholesome; and I have met with so much kindness and so much learning – not hackneyed and trivial but deep, accurate, ancient, Latin and Greek, that (except for the curiosity of seeing it), I do not now so much care for Italy. When I hear my Colet, I seem to be listening to Plato himself. In Grocyn, who does not marvel at such a perfect round of learning? What can be more acute, profound and delicate than the judgment of Linacre? What has Nature ever created more gentle, more sweet, more happy than the genius of More? I need not go through the list. It is marvellous how general and abundant is the harvest of general learning in this country, to which you ought all the sooner to return.

'I find the climate both pleasant and wholesome'

Oxford and Cambridge were no longer provincial in their curricula, the holdings of their libraries and their outlook; London and the Court, too, were beginning to have a European reputation.

Soon after Erasmus's visit, John Colet was appointed Dean of St Paul's. Listening to Savonarola in Florence, he had seen the power of pulpit oratory, and was fired to follow the vocation of an evangelist. He, too, would declare war on corruption and abuses. His own wealth troubled him, for his father had

twice served as Lord Mayor of London, and he vowed to live simply, content with one frugal meal a day and a plain black robe. Though lay rector of a Suffolk parish from a tender age and a canon of York Minster, it was not until his return from Italy that Colet was ordained. Once more in Oxford, he delivered a series of lectures on St Paul's Epistles which achieved 'a revolution in the academic exposition of the Bible'; moreover he lectured without fee. For Colet the New Testament was not a collection of texts, but a living document, and he was at pains to point out the relevance of scriptural teaching to everyday life in a way which seemed an utter novelty. The divine word was shown to be as relevant to the age of the first Tudor as to the reign of the first Augustus, and the effect on Colet's audiences was electric. Coming as a man of much learning to the Bible, he saw no real problems and was convinced that generations of theologians had posed difficulties in interpretation that simply did not exist; the parable of the mote and the beam was most apposite, for the schoolmen had failed to see the wood for the trees.

Once he became Dean of St Paul's in 1503, thanks to William Warham's influence with King Henry, Colet could zealously develop the technique of his Oxford lectures for his sermons in the Cathedral. The leading 'Oxford Reformer' took London by storm and his sermons inspired the courtier and the man in the street no less than his academic lectures had amazed the University's intelligentsia. Outwardly orthodox, his teaching questioned sacrosanct beliefs and ideas, and this proved heady wine for the young. As he spoke, there were flashes of understanding as if the curtains were parted to show the forthcoming drama of the Reformation; there were moments when comprehension and apprehension dawned. The fact that within the next generation the English were to be termed 'the People of the Book' owes most to Colet's preaching on the Bible. It was an uphill struggle since Warham, Bishop of London and Master of the Rolls, rose in the royal service as Archbishop of Canterbury and Lord Chancellor, and his successor as bishop, Richard Fitz James, could understand neither Colet nor his approach to his task, and misunderstanding bred contempt, hatred even. The Chapter of St Paul's as of custom expected their Dean to bestow reasonable if not lavish entertainment, especially if he

OPPOSITE A portrait of Erasmus by Quentin Metsys.

137

commanded a private income, so Colet's abstemiousness was unpopular. Conversation, not the menu, was for the new Dean the first priority. As Erasmus noted, 'When the requirements of nature, if not of pleasure, had been satisfied, he would start some other topic; and then bade farewell to his guests refreshed in mind as well as in body, and better men at leaving than they came, though with stomachs *not* over-loaded!' Erasmus, who chose Colet as his confessor, was aware that the Reformation in England had already begun.

Colet's father had died a rich man in 1505 leaving the Dean his sole heir, for his other ten sons and eleven daughters had all died. The reformer was convinced that if the world were to be set on the paths of righteousness this could be achieved only by the rising generation being nurtured in the right way. Education, accordingly, became almost an obsession with him and in 1509, as Henry VII lay dying, he used his considerable fortune in founding St Paul's School, in which 153 boys could be taught free. 'My intent is by this school especially to increase knowledge and of worshipping of God and our Lord Jesus Christ, and good Christian life and manners in the children', he wrote in the statutes. He gave the school in trust to the Mercers' Company, which has continued to administer the endowments and form the governing body down the centuries.

Religion came first. Over the desk of the high master was an image of Jesus as a child, shown in the act of teaching, with the inscription above it 'Hear Him'. Each boy was required to salute the image on entering the schoolroom. Prayers were said three times a day and when the boys attended the Cathedral on Sundays and holy days they were to walk in crocodile repeating the penitential psalms. Colet himself compiled a catechism for them, in which they were instructed by the chaplain; this included the Apostles' Creed and the Ten Commandments in English (ominous step) as well as in Latin. There were brief statements on the sacraments, exhortations to loving charity and a miscellaneous collection of precepts touching the good life, including the importance of frequent washing as well as of avoiding unseemly language. Grammar, in the widest sense of the term, was the second subject on the time-table. Colet always admired Cicero as his master of Latin prose but when his friend Linacre, at his invitation, wrote a Latin Grammar it was rejected as too difficult for novices and instead William Lyly, the first high master, produced a grammar which remained a standard text book for generations. St Paul's School, the first modern foundation, revolutionised education and provided a model for a long list of sixteenth-century institutions. But as the prototype it alone embodied the New Learning and the ideals of the Oxford Reformers. The roll call of its pupils included the names of many who left their mark in the annals of Church and State during the seminal years of the English Reformation.

Erasmus, a wandering scholar in the medieval tradition, moving freely from university to university, always regarded England as his spiritual home and looked on Colet as his chief master and More as his greatest friend. Colet's attack on hypocrisy, worldliness and superstition had been made with the heart, and now Erasmus stormed the bastions of outworn orthodoxy with his mind, developing into a systematic argument all the pent-up irritations with the old order. He ridiculed the way in which the writings of Aquinas, Duns Scotus and the other medieval schoolmen had been treated with as much blind respect as if they had been Holy Writ. 'We have been disputing for ages', Erasmus wrote, 'whether the grace by which God loves us and the grace by which we love God are one and the same grace. ... Entire lives have been wasted on these speculations, and men quarrel, curse and come to blows about them.' Erasmus urged men to liberate the human mind from the prison of a reactionary system of thought that was absolutely irrelevant to the modern age. 'All this stuff, of which we know nothing and are not required to know anything, the schoolmen treat as the citadel of our faith.' These were uncomfortable words for those with vested interests in maintaining the old order, but they could not be silenced. The future lay with the Erasmians. More revolutionary than all Martin Luther's teaching, the attitude of Erasmus of Rotterdam had been shaped by the 'Oxford Reformers' of Henry Tudor's England.

Henry had visited Oxford early in his reign, presenting forty oak trees towards the rebuilding of the University Church of St Mary, and his visit may have had something to do with weaning Oxford from persistent Yorkist sympathies, for Lambert Simnel had been born here. Prince Arthur stayed at

Foundations in Oxford and Cambridge

Although Henry VII himself made no new endowments at the universities, his mother and many of his leading courtiers were generous benefactors. At Oxford, Magdalen College had been founded by William Waynflete, Bishop of Winchester in 1448, but building work continued beyond the end of the century. The great bell tower was still incomplete when Prince Arthur stayed at Magdalen in 1501. The other new Oxford College of this period was Corpus Christi, founded by Bishop Fox as a centre of the New Learning. At Cambridge Lady Margaret endowed two colleges with the help of her confessor, John Fisher. She refounded Christ's in 1505, and four years later she secured the suppression of the Augustinian Hospital of St John's to found a college of the same name.

RIGHT The entrance gateway to Christ's College, which is decorated by the arms of Lady Margaret and her son, Henry VII. The royal arms of England are supported by two yales, flanked by the crowned Tudor rose and Beaufort portcullis.

BELOW The bell tower of Magdalen College, Oxford, built while Thomas Wolsey was bursar.

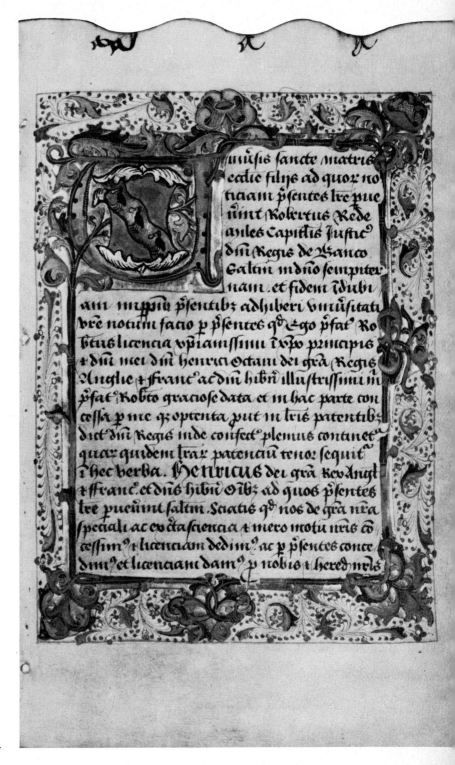

RIGHT Document
recording the foundation
of Christ's College,
Cambridge by Lady
Margaret Beaufort in 1505.

Magdalen in 1501, where the bell tower begun under Thomas Wolsey's bursarship was still incomplete. But, thanks largely to John Fisher's influence with the Lady Margaret, Cambridge was much closer to King and Court than Oxford. The provost of King's College, Cambridge, John Argentine, was physician to both Princes Arthur and Henry. In Cambridge, as at Oxford, the small medieval halls of residence for undergraduates were in decline and the future lay with the colleges which were annexing many of the halls and looked with envious eyes on monastic foundations. As we have noticed, Godshouse became transformed under Lady Margaret Beaufort's direction into Christ's College. Jesus College, established by Bishop Alcock of Ely, briefly tutor to Edward v, was the only entirely new foundation of these years, though most of the endowments came from a suppressed monastery. Other benefactors were making plans, such as William Smith and Richard Fox, who early in the next reign founded Brasenose and Corpus Christi Colleges at Oxford. The new collegiate system was well established before the upheaval of the Reformation.

King Henry had been concerned about the state of the clergy's morals long before Dean Colet had condemned 'the abominable impiety' of certain priests 'who fear not to rush from the bosom of some foul harlot into the temple of the Christ'. In his first Parliament a royal bill had been presented to require every bishop to proceed by canon law against incontinent priests and monks. We know from a visitation of the Welsh dioceses of Bangor and St David's, in which Henry took a keen interest, that no fewer than eighty celibate priests kept mistresses. In 1490 he told Pope Innocent VIII that the decline in monastic observances had become scandalous and he secured a papal bull which empowered Cardinal Morton to make visitations of the religious houses throughout the province of Canterbury and to see that reforms were made. As a result various priors were removed from office for mismanagement. By a later bull Henry set in train an investigation of the separate orders of friars, whose numbers had seriously dwindled. He did not doubt for one moment that, properly ordered, the religious houses and the friaries, great and small, played a significant role in the spiritual life of England. The idea of dissolving the monasteries and appropriating their wealth was completely

142

alien to his cast of mind and, indeed, the most significant of all Henry's benefactions was to Westminster Abbey.

He was concerned that heresy should be extirpated, though only a tiny handful of the ninety-three men and women accused of being heretics in his reign (most of them for Lollard tendencies) were sent to the stake; one heretic was actually converted by the King from his errors at the stake in Canterbury in 1498. Like other Christian monarchs, he gave lip service to the idea of Crusades against the infidel and in 1507 he proposed to Pope Julius II that a fresh Crusade should be undertaken since he had 'always been inclined to shed the blood of the enemies of the Christian faith and to reconquer the Holy Sepulchre'. Unfortunately Crusades, like other forms of warfare, were costly. The King maintained a collecting-box at Court, much as a modern parent places one or more charity boxes on his hall table; but when the royal box was opened by the papal envoy there was no more than £11. 11s. in it 'which result made our hearts sink within us, for there were present the King, the Queen, the mother of the King, the mother of the Queen, besides dukes, earls and marquesses, and other lords and ambassadors, so that we had expected to have had much more'. Henry himself had no sympathy with anti-clericalism, once he had established the right to remove political offenders from sanctuary, since clerics were the necessary buttresses of his own lay administration at every level. Dean Colet was one of the very few men to reach high ecclesiastical office who had not served in embassies or the civil service.

From the early years of the fifteenth century traders sailing from Bristol, King's Lynn and Hull had gone to Iceland in search of fish, but before Henry's accession the Hanseatic merchants from the German ports had largely ousted the English. It seems to us a familiar story: there had been intense rivalry and many felt that the Icelandic waters were being disastrously over-fished. The men of Bristol, anxious to find alternative fishing grounds to meet a growing demand for salted cod and ling, in and out of Lent, pushed further into the Atlantic. In July 1480, twelve years before Columbus's westward voyage, two vessels, the *George* and the *Trinity*, sailed from Bristol 'not for the purpose of trading, but to seek and discover a certain island

'To seek and discover a certain island called the Isle of Brasil'

called the Isle of Brasil' – a land which lay in the western part of Ireland, according to Master Lloyd, 'the most scientific mariner of all England'. Two months later the little ships were driven by storms into a haven in Ireland, their expedition at an end, yet the men were undaunted and the next year made a further attempt, though their voyage was equally fruitless. The misty sea-lore about Greenland, known to the map-makers, and even lands beyond, was an established part of the vernacular traditions which mariners mulled over in the quayside taverns. An Italian named Christopher Columbus, who had sailed to Iceland in a Bristol ship, was well aware of the gossip about a continent that lay in the far west, which he and everyone else assumed to be Asia. It is highly likely that certain Bristol fishing-craft had actually reached the Dogger Bank and Nova Scotia by the year 1490, convinced that the land was 'Brasil'.

By then there was feverish activity. Bristol ships were regularly trading with the Portuguese island of Madeira, some Englishmen were adventuring in the service of Spain in the conquest of the Canaries, a thousand miles out in the Atlantic, while a fugitive Portuguese count was at Henry's Court, urging him to encourage trade with North Africa.

It is one of the ironies of history that while Columbus was waiting for the reaction of Ferdinand and Isabella to his pro-posals for an expedition of discovery across the Atlantic, he sent his brother Bartholomew to England to try to attract rival sup-port for his scheme. Bartholomew Columbus had the misfor-tune to fall into the hands of pirates on his way from Spain and it was not until the winter of 1488–9 that he was in London. At that time Henry had his hands full and his revenues com-mitted, for he was about to become involved in a war with France, so he declined to become patron of the projected adven-ture, even though he was already aware of the accepted theory that a westward passage would lead to Asia, the land of spices, fine silks and rich treasure. Thus Columbus sailed under the Spanish flag in 1492.

John Cabot, born in Genoa but subsequently a citizen of Venice, had for a time been resident in Bristol and was possibly there when Henry visited the port in 1486. He knew about the aspirations of local mariners and the record of their en-deavours to find 'Brasil'. He also happened to be in Seville when Columbus returned from 'the Indies' in 1493 and at once appreciated that the Genoese, for all his apparent success, had failed to reach the land that Marco Polo had termed 'Cathay'. Cabot in consequence felt emboldened to find the 'island of Brasil' of the Bristolians, which he assumed must be the north-east cape of Asia. In due course he was back in Bristol to renew contacts with local ship-owners who might give him the financial backing for his proposed venture. Early in 1496 he obtained an audience of King Henry who granted him a comprehensive patent for sailing to all parts of the 'eastern, western and northern sea' for discovering 'whatso-ever islands, countries', etc, that existed there and 'are un-known to Christians'. These territories were to be occupied in Henry Tudor's name and one fifth of the net profit of the expedition was to go to the crown. The wording of Cabot's patent certainly implies that Columbus had not reached Asia and that his 'Indies' were only a stage on the voyage. By the emphasis on lands 'unknown to Christians', the King took account of Spanish rights in Columbus's discoveries and paid lip service to Pope Alexander VI's bull of 1493 which divided 'the New World' between the monarchs of Spain and Portugal. For an orthodox King, such as Henry, it was an imperative duty, he claimed, to conquer and convert lands held by infidels.

Cabot's first attempt, in 1496, was unsuccessful, for he was forced back, yet he left Bristol a second time in the *Matthew* on 20 May 1497 and on 24 June he sighted The New Found Land – very possibly the shore of Nova Scotia. He went ashore to erect a cross, together with the banners of Henry VII, the Pope and St Mark of Venice, but he avoided all contact with the natives. The *Matthew* was back in Bristol, thanks to favourable winds, on 6 August, when the Bristol men from the crew reported to their fellows ashore that 'they could bring thence so many fish that they would have no further need of Iceland'. When Cabot rode to London he was mobbed as 'the great admiral'.

This was a critical year for Henry, with the pretender War-beck still at large in the west and trouble on the Scottish border, but he gave Cabot another audience and listened to his claims to have discovered Asia and his fervent hopes for the develop-ment of a new route for the spice trade that would make London rival Lisbon as a mart for pepper. For the present he gave Cabot

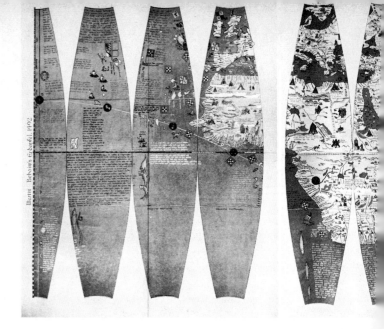

Christopher Columbus

Columbus was born in Genoa in the late 1440s. He served as a sailor in his youth, and also engaged in trade in Genoa as a weaver. In 1492 he made his first voyage westwards under the patronage of Ferdinand and Isabella, landing in the New World in October. He arrived back in Spain the following spring, and was received with great splendour at Barcelona by their Catholic Majesties.

ABOVE RIGHT Martin Behaim's Globe of the World, 1492, drawn before Columbus's discoveries were known.
RIGHT A detail from the same globe.

OPPOSITE A seventeenth-century engraving of the departure of Columbus from Santa Fé in April 1492. He is being seen off by Ferdinand and Isabella.

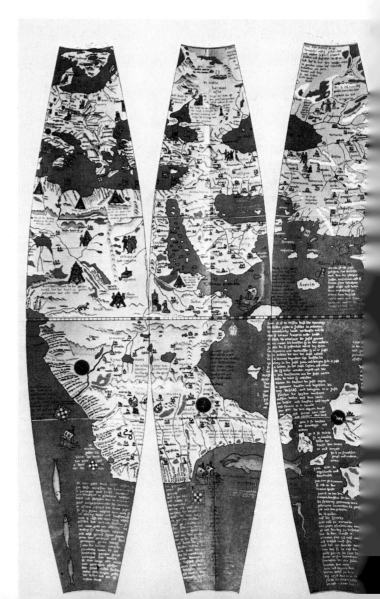

146

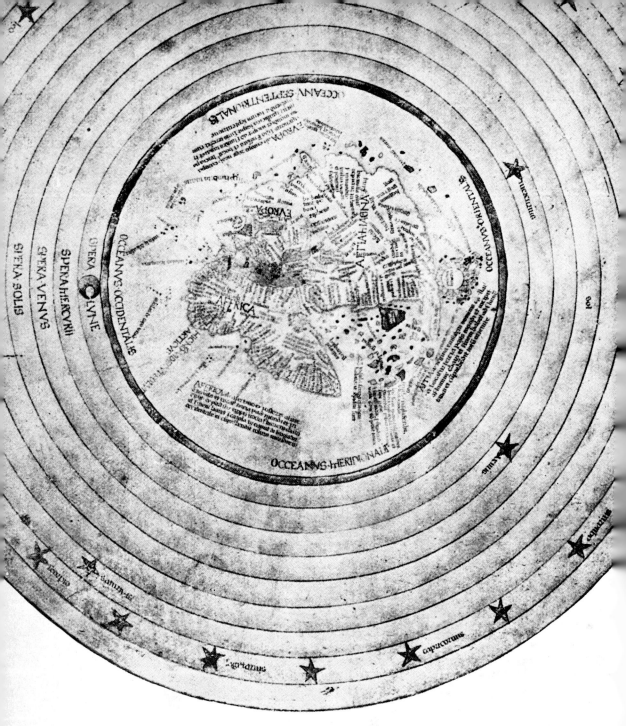

ABOVE Columbus's conception of the world: 'the earth is a sphere in the centre of nine celestial spheres, the Continents forming an island in the middle of four oceans.'

OPPOSITE Copy of the Book of Privileges (Titles) conferred upon Christopher Columbus by Ferdinand and Isabella on the return from his first voyage in 1493. The title of Don was presented to himself and his brothers, and he was served and saluted as a grandee of Spain.

Eſilla muy noble.

En muy leal çibdad de ſeuilla. miercoles quatro
dias del mes de Enero (año del naſçimyento
de nro Saluador ihū xpō de mill e quinientos
e dos años. En eſte dicho dia e ora de
biſperas poco mas o menos. eſtando en la poſada
del ſeñor almirante delas yndias que es en eſta
dicha çibdad en la collaçion de ſancta maria) ante eſteuan dela fca
e fernando ffuiſ monteros alldes ordinarios en eſta dicha çibdad de ſuſo
por el Rey e la Reyna nros ſeñores. E en preſença de mi martin
rodriguez eſcriuano publico deſta dicha çibdad de ſeuilla e delos teſti-
gos yuſo eſcriptos que a ello fueron preſentes. pareçio enel preſente
almuy magnifico ſeñor. Don xpoual colon. Almirante mayor
del mar oceano. viſo Rey e gouernador delas yſlas e tra firme.
E preſento antel dicho alldes çiertas cartas e prouiſiones e çedulas
delos dichos Rey e Reyna nros ſeñores. eſcriptas en papel e pargamino
e firmadas de ſus reales nonbres. E ſelladas con ſus ſellos de
plomo pendientes en filos de ſeda de colores. E de çera colo-
rada en las eſpaldas. E refrendadas de çiertos oficiales de ſu real
caſa. Segund por ellas e por cada una dellas pareçia. El thenor
delas quales una en pos de otras es eſte que ſe ſigue. ─── xxxv

El Rey e la Reyna.

ffrn de Soria lugar teniente de nro Almirante mayor de castilla. nos
vos mandamos que les fagades dar a don xpoual colon nro
Almirante de la mar oceano. Un traslado abtorizado en publica forma que
faga fe. de qualeſquier cartas de merçed e priuillegios e confirmaçiones que el
dicho almirante mayor de caſtilla tiene de ſu cargo e oficio de Almirantadgo. onde el y otros por el lieue coſas loſ dreſs e otras coſas a ello
perteneſçientes a nil dho cargo. por que vemos fecho merçed al dho don
xpoual colon que aya coſas las merçedes e honrras e prerrogatiuas
e libertades e derechos e Salarios en el almirantadgo delas yndias
que tiene e coſa del dho nro Almirante mayor en el Almirantadgo
de caſtilla. lo qual fazed coſa dho luego como fuerdes requerido con
eſta nra carta ſyn que a ello pongays eſcuſa ni dilaçion alguna. E
ſy anſi no lo fizierdes compliendo. mandamos al nro Aſiſtente
e otros juſtiçias dela çibdad de ſeuilla que vos apremien a que
lo aſi fazer e cunplir. E non fagades ni fagan ende al. fecha en la
çibdad de burgos. a veynt e tres dias del mes de Abril de
noueçientos e ſeys años. yo el Rey. yo la Reyna. Juan mudela.

a modest reward and later assigned him a pension; the entry in the royal household accounts laconically ran, 'To him that found the new isle – £10'. During that winter John Day, an Englishman in Andalusia, wrote to Columbus, giving him information he had gathered about Cabot's voyage, and in his letter he said 'it is considered certain that the Cape of the said land was discovered in the past by the men from Bristol'. Yet the King was cautiously optimistic and when John Cabot again set out in May 1498, he provided one of the five ships in the expedition, that were laden with English cloth and other articles for trade. Cabot never returned from this voyage.

Even with Vasco da Gama's voyage round the Cape of Good Hope, the English still maintained their strong interest in the north Atlantic route. Each year Henry rewarded various Bristol merchant adventurers, such as Robert Thorne and Hugh Elyot, whose ships returned from 'the New Found Land', bringing modest offerings to Court from his new empire. A servant of Sir Walter Herbert came to present the King with 'a brasil bow and two red arrows', while another paraded three natives dressed in skins. Henry must have been acutely disappointed that these voyages were not more profitable, that the attempt at colonisation had failed; one is reminded of his grand-daughter's disappointment at Raleigh's Roanoke voyages and the fate of the first Virginian colony. Ferdinand of Spain could boast of the wealth of his West Indies, and the King of Portugal of the rich cargoes of pepper and cloves that came to the Tagus, but England had so far found only cod. At least Henry had not completely missed the boat, like the King of France, and he remained to the end convinced that the effort to establish a new trade route to Asia was worth full encouragement. Sebastian Cabot, who had sailed on the 1497 voyage, persisted with his father's quest for a North-West Passage and at the close of Henry's reign discovered Hudson Strait (as modern research has made clear) and possibly part of Hudson's Bay as well, though he did not return to England until the next reign.

Oceanic discovery had become an essential element in Henry VII's policy and for this he risked antagonising the Spaniards and Portuguese. Even the maps of the New World produced by Spanish cartographers showed a lengthy stretch of coast under the English flag, with the legend *'mare descubierto por inglese'* ('sea discovered by the English'), and in 1501 Ferdinand and Isabella had ordered a flotilla to be sent from the Spanish bases in Central America towards the north, to set up marks with the royal arms of Aragon and Castile 'so that you may stop the exploration of the English in that direction'. The voyages of the Cabots and their Bristol friends had been made under royal patronage and once Henry died this particular phase of English exploration ended. The young Henry VIII was not interested in the North-West Passage and with the lack of a King's support, fresh enterprise ceased, though 'Newland' cod and ling had by then become a regular feature of Englishmen's diet.

and Country 1485-1509

Henry's England was a small kingdom of no more than three million subjects, of whom some sixty thousand lived in the capital – the combined yet still separated cities of London and Westminster. No provincial city approached London in population or wealth, for York, Bristol, Coventry, Norwich and Plymouth each had less than ten thousand people living within their walls. London was the hub of the kingdom's commercial activity, just as Westminster was the seat of government, and cordial relations with their citizens were fundamental to the success of the new dynasty. 'Tudor despotism', it has been said, 'consisted largely in London's dominance over the rest of the kingdom.'

The Scottish poet William Dunbar, coming to London from the small, provincial city of distant Edinburgh towards the end of the century, was amazed at the splendour as well as the size of England's capital. Here, he thought, was a new Troy, truly an international centre, bustling with activity, well-governed, its daily life punctuated by civic pomp. Its bridge over the river, the port, the Tower, the churches, public buildings and private houses all attracted his most favourable comment; London was not just a grand metropolis, he considered, but a beautiful place – a 'sweet paradise pre-excelling in pleasure':

> London, thou art of townes *A per se.*
> Soveraign of cities, seemliest in sight,
> Of high renown, riches and royaltie;
> Of lordis, barons, and many a goodly knyght;
> Of most delectable lusty ladies bright;
> Of famous prelates, in habitis clericall;
> Of merchauntis full of substance and of myght;
> London, thou art the flour of Cities all.
>
> Gladdith anon, thou lusty Troynovaunt
> Citie that some tyme elaped was New Troy;
> In all the erth, imperiall as thou stant,
> Pryncesse of townes, of pleasure and of joy,
> A richer restith under no Christen roy:
> For manly Power, with craftis naturall,
> Fowrmeth none fairer sith the flode of Noy:
> London, thou art the flour of Cities all.

The English people in 1485 were still very far from being a nation. Local loyalties to powerful land-owners persisted; in

154

London.

London in 1510: the earliest printed view of the City, produced by Richard Pynson in his *Chronycle of Englonde*. In the centre is the spire of Old St Paul's, with London Bridge and the Tower of London to the right, and Ludgate in front.

the North country, for instance, they 'knew no lord but a Percy', and civil war had accentuated this particularist attitude. Regional differences remained very striking, whether it was in speech or methods of farming, the shape of church towers or diet, the kind of cloth woven or the veneration of particular saints. The Tudor sovereigns would succeed in welding their subjects into a nation during the next hundred years, but Henry began the process by curbing the power of his barons, ending the days of private armies of retainers. His son would bring Wales properly into the English administrative system and his elder daughter's marriage would lead to the union with Scotland, though Ireland was to remain a special problem. Only Calais survived from a great empire in France; yet for all her isolation England was still very much part of Europe, her Church subject to the Pope and to the intricate code of canon law. Within the kingdom the separate system of Church courts was divisive: on the one hand the ecclesiastical courts exempted clerks in holy orders (roughly speaking the literate) from the jurisdiction of the King's courts, and on the other, they governed such important aspects of the lives of lay men and women as matrimonial affairs and the probate of wills. It was surprising that anticlericalism was not much stronger.

Agricultural scene: a woodcut by Sebastian Brandt from his version of Virgil's *Georgics*, printed in Strasbourg in 1502.

An Italian who visited England just before the turn of the century has left a vivid picture of the state of the kingdom. Compared with his native Italy, which was being trampled over by French armies, this was, indeed, a flourishing realm – rich, fertile and plentiful in natural resources, though underpopulated. Despite London's size, England was essentially an agricultural country, a land 'all diversified by pleasant undulating hills and beautiful valleys, there being nothing to be seen but agreeable woods, extensive meadows or lands in cultivation and the greatest plenty of water springing everywhere'. Except for the walled cities, there was not much distinction (on other than legal grounds) between town and country and most of the market towns were no more than overgrown villages which had acquired rights to hold markets and fairs. He was amazed at the range of luxuries on sale in London, where Cheapside alone boasted fifty-two goldsmiths' shops. All the people he met were well-dressed and were partial to their food almost to the extent of gluttony. Their language he thought 'extremely polite' and their way of speaking it a relief from the harsh tones of Flemish and German. He also praised everyday manners – a surprising compliment for a polished Italian:

They have the incredible courtesy of remaining with their heads uncovered, with an admirable grace, whilst they talk to each other . . . although their dispositions are somewhat licentious, I never have noticed any one, either at court or amongst the lower orders, to be in love; whence one must necessarily conclude, either that the English are the most discreet lovers in the world, or that they are incapable of love. I say this of the men, for I understand it is quite the contrary with the women, who are very violent in their passions. Howbeit the English keep a very jealous guard over their wives, though any thing may be compensated in the end by the power of money.

Erasmus, first visiting England when he was thirty, was in raptures about the peculiarly English habit of kissing: 'Wherever you go', he told a Flemish friend, 'you are received with kisses from everybody. … People arrive: kisses; they depart: kisses. Wherever people foregather there are lots of kisses; in fact whatever way you turn everything is full of kisses. Oh,

Faustus, if you had once tasted how soft, how delicious those kisses are.'

Parents were shy of showing affection towards their children, and the warm-hearted Italian was shocked at the early age (certainly by the time the child was nine) at which both girls and boys were sent away from home to other households to continue their upbringing and begin apprenticeships.

If in general the English were stingy in money matters they were far from mean in their alms-giving at Mass, which many attended daily. (It was another Italian who a few years back had written 'In the morning they are as devout as angels; after dinner they are like devils.') Their antipathy to foreigners was in marked contrast to the open friendliness of the Scots, for they were deeply suspicious that merchants came to their island only 'to make themselves masters of it and to usurp their goods'. Patriotism was strong. 'They think that there are no other men than themselves and no other world but England and whenever they see a handsome foreigner they say that "He looks like an Englishman" and that "It is a great pity that he should not be an Englishman".' They behaved, indeed, 'as if England were the whole world'. Altogether our Italian was a kindly and sympathetic observer. Despite the rain which in some years fell every day in summer, the climate was temperate and the inhabitants remarkably healthy, with men and women, 'of all ages handsome and well-proportioned'. Such were the idyllic impressions of Henry's realm and subjects as the fifteenth century gave way to the sixteenth, and they need some correction.

The shape of the country differed in many respects from the England of the 1970s. The Fens had not yet been drained, Purbeck and Portland in Dorset were still islands off the mainland, the Suffolk coast jutted further into the sea. There were remarkably few good roads and some of these were in part impassable after heavy rains. A man's most valued possession was his horse and ladies who did not care for the rough and tumble of riding side-saddle on bumpy ways stayed at home, for there were no carriages. England was still a land of many trees, for although the area of the royal forests had been contracting as men had nibbled at the waste over two and a half centuries, there were extensive areas remaining in Hampshire, Wiltshire, Gloucestershire and Nottinghamshire that provided oak for ships' timbers

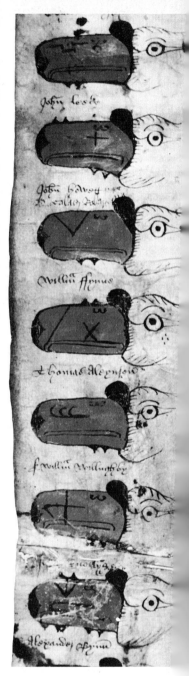

Swanmarks from a roll of the distinctive marks upon the bills of swans belonging to various people in

Lincolnshire and Cambridgeshire, from 1497 to 1507 with additions dated 1515.

and cover for the red and fallow deer, as well as for the wild boar and the foxes that attacked them.

It was reckoned 'a truly beautiful thing to behold one or two thousand swans upon the River Thames'. These royal swans, marked in the bill with two nicks, were jealously guarded and by an Act of Parliament of 1496 anyone stealing eggs from swans' nests was liable to imprisonment for a year and a day and to be fined at the King's pleasure. Rolls of swanmarks were compiled, such as the one illustrated on the left, to show ownership of the birds in other rivers and marshes. Nature had endowed England with a wonderful river system, with small craft plying on tributaries far from the sea and these waterways made up for the lack of good roads.

The diet, even for the well-to-do, was unbalanced and for the poor was monotonous. At the rich man's table a great variety of game and fowl was served in season; venison was plentiful and swans, peacocks, herons, mallards, teals, larks and smaller birds featured on the menu. While the peasant's wife stirred her stewpot, the noble's lady planned intricate pies and pastries, for almost every kind of meat and game could be combined into a pie. Fish, fresh and salt, came in profusion, though many of these dishes must have tasted alike. It is hard to imagine a diet, even for a king, so starved of fresh vegetables; cabbages, cauliflowers and broccoli were not yet grown in England and the potato would not be introduced for almost another century. Salads were common in summer, but these consisted largely of lettuces, cucumber, onions and nuts, dressed with herbs and the 'salat oil' that came from Spain. With spices so expensive, the herb garden had a special significance and every townsman with a plot of ground grew mint, parsley, thyme, chives, basil and rosemary for the kitchen. The lack of potatoes and rice made for an enormous consumption of bread.

For three-quarters of the population bread was truly the 'staff of life'. Bad harvests meant famine and the strong likelihood of numbers of people being starved to death. While the more affluent ate a whitish loaf, made from a mixture of wheat and barley, the great body of the King's subjects fed on black or dark brown bread, made from rye and barley, known as 'maslin'; to eke out the flour bin in times of shortage peasants would add oats, peas and beans. Already in Henry's reign

159

cargoes of rye were being imported from the Baltic by the Hanseatic merchants.

Meat, if not a luxury, was seldom fresh. People survived the winter months on smoked bacon and salted beef, and if Lenten fasting had not been ordained for religious reasons it would still have been a natural requirement through the lack of meat supplies in the late winter. The poor peasant made ends meet only as a result of the fringe benefits of rural life – not merely the opportunity of gathering nuts, fruit and berries, but the chance of poaching rabbits, hares, fish and, with luck, one of his lord's fallow deer; enquiries before the forest justices so often ended in an unidentifiable culprit. Most country folk knew the art of netting birds and the ways of the wild fowler. Near the coast and the many rivers there was an abundance of fish. Cheese and eggs were staple foods all the year round and, in the absence of sugar, the need for honey led to widespread bee-keeping. The lack of fresh vegetables was in part overcome by the availability of fruit – apples, pears and plums in particular, though strawberries and soft fruit were also grown. Every child went nutting round the hedgerows in the autumn.

Landowners, great and small, brewed their own ale – the headier beer was unknown in England – and the mistress of the house made her own cider and traditional cordials. (This was a world still without tea, coffee and chocolate.) Children drank small beer or porter, even for breakfast. The wine trade with Gascony, which had been built up to a considerable volume during English rule, continued unabated, filling the cellars of the merchants of Bristol and King's Lynn who specialised in this trade. In the larger towns every tenth shop was a tavern selling wine and on days of national or civic celebration fountains of wine were set up in market-places for by-standers and in the courtyards of stately homes for tenants to take their fill.

The expectation of life was grim, with so many people only just above the subsistence level, suffering from acute malnutrition. As always, health was not merely a question of money or rank, though full purses and a title could obtain the best medical advice to be had and the most likely 'cures'. Dean Colet was the only baby out of the twenty-two born to his mother who survived childhood, even though their father was a Lord Mayor of London. Henry VII's own experience of parenthood was

OPPOSITE Hanse merchants in the port of Hamburg, from a miniature of 1497.

perhaps better than that of most of his subjects, for three of his seven children outlived him, while Elizabeth of York, like so many mothers, never recovered from her last confinement. The state of medicine and surgery meant that there was no hope for the physically weak, no help for the crippled, the poor-sighted and the accident-prone. Coroners' inquests show how frequently farm labourers who were kicked by a horse or had a foot crushed under a cart-wheel never recovered. The partnership of a marriage was, on the face of it, unlikely to endure for more than fifteen years or so, for by then one of the couple would have died, and the chances are that at any time nearly half the adult population was widowed and embarking on a second, or later, marriage. Perhaps the pledge required by the Church, that marriage lasted until death, was so readily taken and divorce so rarely resorted to, simply because nature had fixed a medium term to every marriage. Child marriages were not uncommon among the land-owning classes, even if the young couple continued to live apart for a few years, but most men could not hope to marry until they had served out their apprenticeship to a gild or acquired a farm holding; apprenticeship indentures categorically forbade marriage.

'The plague, pestilence and sudden death' of the Litany, even if it was said in the Latin of the Church, was a phrase of spine-chilling relevance to everyone who heard it. The terrors of the Black Death of 1348–51 which had more than decimated the population were part of the national folk-memory. Pestilences of one kind or another returned sporadically during the fifteenth century, but there was no widespread infection with chronic effects. Any sudden epidemic was branded 'the plague'. The sweating sickness, though less terrifying than the bubonic plague, made its début in London in 1485 and was soon reckoned a most serious infection, even if the first visitation caused comparatively few deaths. It would continue to return most summers, increasing in intensity. London and the larger provincial cities were the most vulnerable to these attacks and Henry started the habit, faithfully followed by his successors, of leaving London during the warmest months for the safer air of his rural houses. Among infectious diseases that could prove fatal was measles and early in the reign there was an outbreak of 'the measles so strong and in especial among the ladies and

The transitory nature of life was all too clear to Englishmen in the late fifteenth century, and their obsession with death and the afterlife is probably a result of this. Most people of prominence and wealth made endowments in their wills for charities to be set up and masses to be said for their souls. This late fifteenth-century embroidered fragment shows Thomas Smyth and his wife Joan praying, and the inscription asks the reader to pray for their souls.

the gentlewomen that some died of that sickness'. Leprosy had by now been mercifully eradicated and the isolation hospitals for lepers, like St James's in the park at Westminster, were used as old people's homes. Syphilis was unknown in England.

Despite Dunbar's praises, the stench of London, particularly in hot weather, must have been intolerable. Masters of City livery companies invariably carried nosegays as they walked in procession in an age in which sanitation and other problems of public health were left to chance. The gutter was everyone's dustbin and some people's sewer. Yet London, York and Bristol were no worse in this respect than Paris, Rome or Cologne. A further hazard for town-dwellers was fire and, with so many of the smaller houses being built of timber and thatched, it is remarkable that there were so few conflagrations.

England was predominantly a rural society. Most of King Henry's subjects earned their living from the land, and agriculture remained, as it always had been, the principal industry. The fall in the population from the level before the Black Death coupled with the extent of land available for cultivation had improved the peasant's lot so that this seemed a veritable golden age. The French peasant, it was said, went barefoot, but the Englishman was well shod. No one in England, wrote Sir John Fortescue, drank water except out of religious devotion or penitential zeal. Yet already in Henry's reign a natural increase in the population was bringing pressure on the land, forcing up prices, and soon tenants were having to bid against each other to offer higher rents to new-style landlords, who had invested their profits from commerce in broad acres. A considerable enclosure of open fields and of common lands was in progress. By agreement, tenants exchanged their strips in the open fields so that they could consolidate their holdings in a rational way, since moving from strip to strip at every stage of the farming year was exceedingly time-wasting and ill-suited to a commercialised approach to agriculture. Within many manors the commons were being parcelled out in the same spirit. The enclosure movement varied in pace from district to district and the process would not be completed until the age of the Georges, but in these early years, with few statutory controls, the race was to the swift. Of course the grasping, quick-witted individual outdid his fair-minded and less suspicious neighbours. Thomas Tusser had an apposite verse:

> The poor at enclosing do grutch
> Because of abuses that fall,
> Lest some man should have but too much,
> And some again nothing at all.

There was, then, the beginning of a great reshuffling of property at grass-roots level long before the upheaval caused by the Dissolution of the Monasteries. Developments in sheep-farming, too, were producing rapid changes in the countryside.

For over a century the country had been experiencing a minor industrial revolution, and the chief manufacture of the kingdom was now woollen cloth; the finished product had ousted the raw material, wool, as England's staple export. The domestic demand for wool for the clothiers had altered the character of farming in various districts. In Oxfordshire and Gloucestershire lay landlords like the Stonors and monastic landlords such as the abbots of Oseney and Winchcombe, had abandoned arable farming to turn their demesne lands into sheep runs, while in parts of Warwickshire the enclosure of open fields for large-scale sheep farming had led to the decay of several peasant communities. One shepherd with a couple of dogs could oversee the flocks on the grassland which had hitherto provided work under the plough for a score of men. The government aimed at preventing further depopulation by passing an Act in 1489 'in restraint of sheep-farming' and the preamble to it mentioned the evils arising from the destruction of farmhouses and the conversion of arable to pasture. As a further attempt at control, the King forbade all export of wool without his specific licence and special powers were given to the Company of Merchants of the Staple with their headquarters at Calais. Yet the shortage of English wool available for sale on the Continent provoked widespread smuggling and the first Enclosure Act of 1489 could not be effectively enforced. A large-scale enquiry made in 1517 into depopulation and enclosures certainly showed a great number of evictions over the previous generation, though by no means all of these enclosures were made in pursuit of 'the golden fleece'. Under the impetus of quick profits, certain parts of England were being brought to the condition where 'sheep devoured men'.

In the clothing industry there were new-style capitalists like John Tame and his son Edmund, who maintained a large manufactory at Cirencester, making 'Gloucester whites' on their looms, assured of regular supplies of wool from their own flocks that grazed on the Cotswold slopes near Fairford. Another large-scale operator was Thomas Spring from the Suffolk village of Lavenham, whose kerseys had an enviable reputation. It was no accident that Fairford and Lavenham churches, rebuilt at this time, were among the most beautiful in the country. All over the land the growth of what had been essentially a cottage industry encouraged the rise of the middleman clothier, who toured villages buying up finished cloths and took them to London for re-sale.

From the older, corporate towns, where the gilds could enforce restrictive regulations about output and quality, some members of the weaver's craft left for the villages to carry on their work free from close invigilation. Many weavers left Norwich and Bury St Edmunds for places outside the walls where they could wink at the rules. There were, of course, complaints about sub-standard wares, especially of cloth that had been excessively stretched to reach the statutory measurements. The tenter, the large frame on which the finished cloth was stretched (which gives us the phrase 'on tenter hooks') was almost as common a sight in the clothing districts of early Tudor England as the advertisement hoarding is today. The demand for cloth stimulated new processes and there was a natural opposition to many of them from the craft guilds. Shearmen, fearful for their jobs, objected to the use of 'instruments of iron' and in 1495 they succeeded in bringing pressure to bear so that a law was passed requiring that fustian cloths should be shorn with 'the broad shears only'. An early riot, staged on the same principles which would motivate the machine-breaking Luddites of the early nineteenth century, occurred in 1485 when the owner of a fulling mill in the Stroud Valley of Gloucestershire was attacked by a mob intent on murdering him if he did not close down his mill.

The drift from the land to the town and *vice versa* produced the sturdy beggar who had to rely on the charity of the faithful, for poor relief was not yet reckoned a responsibility of the state. Great land-owners, such as the Duke of Buckingham, copied

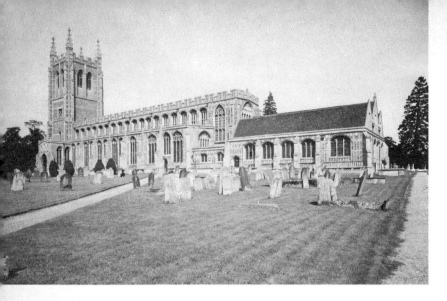

Two tangible records of the wealth accruing from the wool trade in England.
LEFT Long Melford Church is one of the great 'wool cathedrals' built in East Anglia in the fifteenth century, with the wool revenues. The church is built in the Perpendicular style with enormous windows, and is huge for the size of the community it served.

BELOW Paycocke's is a fine timbered merchant's house, built in about 1500 in Coggleshall, Essex, when it was one of the centres of clothmaking in East Anglia, and one of its richest clothiers was John Paycocke. The timbers dividing the upper and lower floors are covered in carvings including the Paycocke trade signs.

the King in appointing an almoner who would provide food and drink for the needy, and every monastery dispensed hospitality at its gates, every church collected alms for distributing to the poor. The medieval system still largely worked. Not for another generation, under the advancing tide of pauperism, would the religious and voluntary agencies prove insufficient and leave the State to intervene by repressing vagrancy.

English looms produced three main types of cloth – the traditional broadcloth now made mostly in Wiltshire and Gloucestershire, which was the most expensive material; the kerseys manufactured in the West Riding of Yorkshire, Suffolk, Kent, Hampshire and Devon, which were less heavy; and the cheaper 'friezes' coming from Lancashire and parts of Wales. Most of the export trade had become centred in London where a regular cloth market was held at Blackwell Hall in Basinghall Street. The traffic here was chiefly in the hands of the English Merchants Adventurers, most of them citizens of London, who until recently had held their Continental mart at Utrecht, where William Caxton had earned a considerable livelihood by dealing in cloth before he turned to printing. Under King Henry, the role of the Adventurers became formalised, for he organised them into a chartered company granting them a monopoly of the trade. Merchants from provincial ports felt they were being unfairly excluded from the profitable Flemish traffic and as a result of their protests the Company was required to reduce by a third the fee of £20 charged for local associates. The King appreciated the importance of a well-organised company for handling the realm's chief exports and such a close-knit body of merchants would prove useful to him in financial affairs; for example, he could rely on the Company to ensure that all their shipments passed properly through the customs house. After considering the possibility of Middleburg as a mart town, the Merchants Adventurers finally settled in Antwerp and their considerable privileges there were reinforced by Henry's *Intercursus Magnus* of 1496 with Maximilian. For just over two years there had been a stoppage of trade when Margaret of Burgundy had refused to surrender the pretender Warbeck, and in retaliation Henry banished Flemish merchants from England and the Adventurers had moved their base to Calais. This interruption of a lively commercial intercourse had proved to each party how essential it was to their livelihood and now it was resumed amid rejoicing in Antwerp. At that time the Cathedral there was being built and to commemorate the treaty Henry presented a fine stained-glass window that has survived the Protestant furies of the sixteenth century and the hazards of later warfare.

Antwerp had been a small, comparatively unimportant port until the English Merchant Adventurers settled there, but it very swiftly grew to become the commercial capital of Europe. German traders looking for English broadcloth brought to Antwerp their metal wares and the wax, pitch and canvas that came from the Baltic lands. Italian silks and velvets were on sale there and in the last year of the century the Portuguese established in Antwerp their principal 'factory' for the sale of spices and oriental goods; and even though a Portuguese cargo of spices was first unloaded in the Port of London in 1503, England continued to acquire sugar, pepper, ginger and cloves through Antwerp. The port became a vast emporium to which England sent its cloths and from which it obtained the great bulk of its imports, the main exception being French wine. In the Burgundian city was opened a Bourse that developed as the chief international money market and the rates of exchange quoted there for guelders, crowns, florins and the other currencies could cause tremors throughout the capitals of Europe. London and Antwerp had swiftly found a special relationship which was to endure until the 1560s. While the Merchant Adventurers' trade with Antwerp flourished, the role of the Staplers handling the wool sales at Calais inevitably contracted. Foreign merchants still came to England, even though the Italian galleys visited Southampton less and less frequently. The Hanseatic merchants from the German and Baltic ports, resident in England, enjoyed very large privileges, even paying smaller customs dues on various commodities than Englishmen, but their activities had been clipped by the rise of Antwerp.

Among other English industries, already with a long history, there were the tin mines of Cornwall and Devon. Their output was greater than ever before and since they were controlled by the 'Stannary' courts, the tinners augmented the revenues of the duchy of Cornwall, which Henry kept to himself. There was lead mining in the Weald of Kent and Sussex, in Derbyshire, Cumberland and the Mendips of Somerset; the Weald, in particular, was the home of the native armament industry where cannons were cast. Coal mined in Durham, Yorkshire and South Wales was already making a minor contribution to the export trade to the Netherlands and Germany as well as satisfying a growing market for cheap fuel in London, Norwich and other towns easily reached by water. Already men worried about the diminishing woodlands. The burning of 'sea coal' – so called because of its transit by Newcastle vessels down the east coast to the Thames – was beginning to pollute London's atmosphere, yet King Henry continued to burn the more costly and less offensive logs. He had not been on the throne many months before the earliest water-powered pump was in use at a colliery near Durham.

England was becoming wealthier, and the King took his cut from the increase in foreign trade through the customs duties which his first Parliament had granted him for life and by the last years of his reign the customs had become the principal branch of his revenue. Increasing prosperity was evident in the spate of new buildings – royal, ecclesiastical and private – that were going up and in the benefactions made to churches and colleges. The silverware purchased by London merchants, whose fathers had been content with pewter, struck the Italian visitor. By then Parliament had forbidden foreign merchants to take out of the country gold, plate and jewels, partly so that they should buy English products, partly because of the belief that such treasure was best kept in the realm as visible financial reserve.

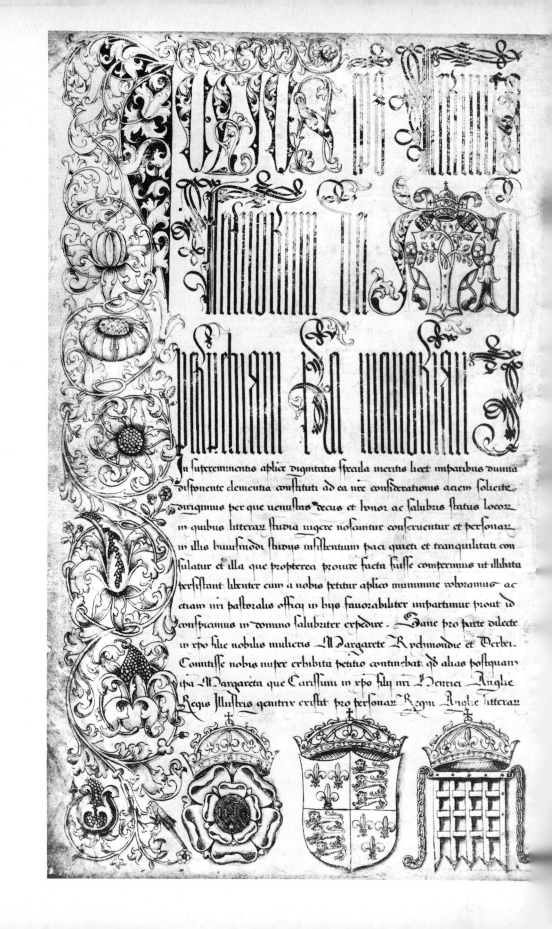

In supreminentis aplice dignitatis fractula meritis licet imparibus diuina
disponente clementia constituti ad ea nre consideracionis aciem solicite
dirigimus per que uenustas decus et honor ac salubris status locox
in quibus litterax studia uigere noscuntur conseruentur et personax
in illis huiusmodi studiis insistentium paci quieti et tranquilitati con
sulatur et illa que propterea prouide facta fuisse comperimus ut illibata
persistant libenter cum a nobis petitur aplico muniumne robramus ac
etiam nri pastoralis officij in hijs fauorabiliter impartimur prout id
conspicimus in domino salubriter expedire. Sane pro parte dilecte
in xpo filie nobilis mulieris Margarete Rychmondie et Derbi.
Comitisse nobis nuper exhibita petitio continebat qd alias postquam
ipsa Margareta que Carissimi in xpo filij nri Henrici Anglie
Regis Illustris genitrix existit pro personax Regni Anglie litterax

7 Royal Power and Administration 1485-1509

HENRY HAD COME to the throne utterly inexperienced in the ways and means of government. He had never sat in Parliament or Council, he had made no study of English law and he was sadly lacking in basic knowledge about royal financial organisation in which he was later to show himself an unparalleled expert. Such unpreparedness for ruling was natural in a King who had spent most of his life in exile in a small duchy with completely different traditions and problems; yet English sovereigns without the disadvantages of exile had come to the throne in the past little better prepared. Henry Tudor was a quick learner and had the benefit of such old hands as Bishop Morton and Reginald Bray. However, he never forgot the disadvantages of his lack of training and was determined that his son Arthur should be better placed, so from the age of ten he was sent to Ludlow under expert tuition to learn the rudiments of government in Wales as an introduction to kingship. His second son, even when he became heir to the throne, was in contrast rather neglected.

Later chroniclers and Henry's first biographer, Francis Bacon, credited him with a detailed political programme for re-establishing royal power and ending by firm rule the internal dissensions of an over-mighty nobility, which had been the plague of England. Such a plan, they detected, was unfolded in the legal and financial reforms which were introduced as the reign progressed, to transform the sovereign into a 'new-style' monarch, attuned to a new dynasty and a new century. This interpretation, which was accepted for a long time, has of late been discredited. Much of Henry's work in fiscal policy, for instance, was not innovation but a return to the methods of Edward IV. In many areas Henry was conservative and there was nothing revolutionary about a fifteenth-century ruler wanting to be authoritarian. Henry's intention in 1485 was simply to win the crown and, having won it, to establish himself by the best means available, improvising and adapting as he gained confidence and experience. Caution and vigilance were among his greatest assets for survival in the 'many years together full of broken seas, tides and tempests'. Had Henry been convinced of the need for radical change, he would have had to take account of the likely outcry from subjects, highborn and lowly; as a foreigner noted, 'if the King should propose to change any old established rule, it would seem to every Englishman as if his life were taken for him'. Government was the art of the possible.

Until the Battle of Stoke had been won, as Henry himself admitted, he was too preoccupied with the everyday tasks of outwitting active and potential rebels to turn to the difficult problems of reforming the Crown estates which 'be greatly fallen into decay'. Financial maladministration had been part of the Lancastrian heritage; in modern parlance the Yorkist kings had proved themselves capable of managing the economy while their opponents had failed disastrously. Sir John Fortescue in his *The Governance of England*, an astute political tract, had recognised the fundamental weakness of the monarchy's financial position, which must be improved if the realm were not to relapse into misgovernment. For Henry, it was no less important to live down the Lancastrian reputation for financial incompetence than to make a permanent solution to the pressing problems. If he was haunted by those 'many secret fears' touching his subjects' personal loyalty to him, he was little less troubled by the fear of insolvency. The margin between success and failure was a narrow one and, for all his carefulness and efficient greed in exploiting the Crown's revenues, he found the expenses of government mounting so that, apart from a reserve of plate and chested treasure, he left no more than £9,100 in cash to his son.

The key institution was the King's Council, a body with supreme administrative powers, which also had a legal jurisdiction. During Henry's reign there was discernible an inner council of senior officials, such as the Chancellor, the Keeper of the Privy Seal, the Treasurer of the Chamber and the King's Secretary, who met frequently, often without the King, to transact a great variety of routine business. An ambassador termed this group of officials the 'secret council' and it bears some resemblance to the 'cabinets' of a much later age. Yet the King was always present when matters of import were being discussed, especially financial and foreign affairs. No one doubted Henry's pre-eminence, and in modern political terms he was his own prime minister. From the Council there had developed a number of subordinate, specialist committees, such as the 'Council Learned in the Law', consisting of legal experts among the Councillors, sitting under the presidency of the Chancellor of the Duchy of Lancaster, first Sir Reginald Bray, and from 1505, Sir Richard Empson. It was largely concerned with enforcing penal statutes, collecting debts due to the Crown with such success that men thought its harshness self-evident.

In other directions, too, Henry and his ministers sought to strengthen the legal system by creating various special tribunals to supplement the work of the ancient common law courts. In part this was necessary since some of the parties were too in-

Administrative organisation under Edward IV, from the black book of his household, 1478.
FAR RIGHT The *Domus regie magnificiencie*, showing the maintenance of the household above stairs, which had to impress the world by its magnificence.
RIGHT In contrast, the *Domus providencis* describes the household below stairs, where providence and prudence included such institutions as the counting house, the bakehouse and the laundry.

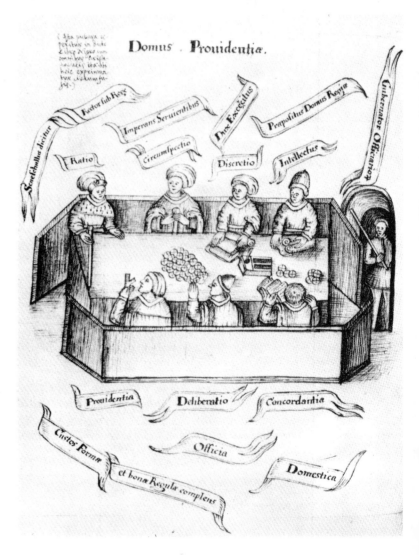

fluential to be amenable to the process of the ordinary courts; in part it was simply pressure of business. A peremptory summons to appear before the King's Council or one of its committees was an effective method of maintaining law and order. Some of these experiments were short-lived, such as the body set up in a moment of panic in 1487 'to try servants of the royal household accused of attempting to destroy the King, his peers and councillors'.

One of the rooms often used for meetings of these special tribunals was a chamber decorated with stars on the ceiling in

Standardisation of Weights and Measures

Among Henry's administrative changes was the standardisation of weights and measures which took place in 1497.

OPPOSITE A chart of the new standards showing the regulation tables for market supervisors.
RIGHT A standard gallon measure of 1496 inscribed 'Henricus Septimus'.
BELOW Wool weights dating from the reign of Henry VII and bearing the arms of England.

176

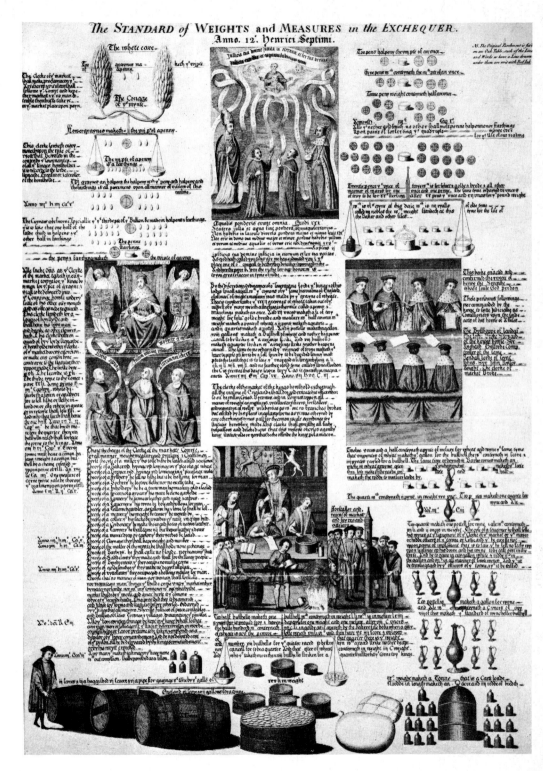

The STANDARD of WEIGHTS and MEASURES in the EXCHEQUER.
Anno. 12. Henrici Septimi.

Two miniature illustrations from a law treatise of the fifteenth century. It is not certain whether the treatise dates from the reign of Henry VI or Henry VII.

LEFT The Court of Common Pleas, showing seven presiding judges, and below them prothonotaries and other officers of the court. On the table are rolls, a closed book and various writing materials. Two ushers with party-coloured robes stand on the table. Before the table stands a

the Palace of Westminster, which came to be known as the Star Chamber. This most famous and much misunderstood tribunal was a conciliar committee established by an Act of 1487 for the summary enforcement of legislation, especially the laws against maintenance and retaining, the corruption of juries, riots and seditions. This body consisted of the Lord Chancellor, the Lord Treasurer, the Keeper of the Privy Seal, a bishop, a lord of the Council and the two chief justices. Years afterwards this committee became termed the Court of Star Chamber, for a clerk

defendant dressed only in his shirt, accompanied by a tipstaff and sergeants. RIGHT The Court of Chancery, presided over by two judges, one tonsured presumably as a priest. On the table stands a clerk in court reading records and an usher, in a party-coloured robe, pressing down the matrix of the Great Seal. In front of him lie folded writs serving as subpoenas and chancery writs. At the bar stand three sergeants with coifs and party-coloured gowns, and lawyers' apprentices.

after Henry's day had added to the entry in the Statute Roll a marginal note – 'pro camera stellata' (for the Starred Chamber). Lawyers and politicians became so certain that the 1487 Act had fathered the summary Court of Star Chamber of Elizabeth I and the early Stuarts, that when the Long Parliament abolished that Court in 1641 it went about repealing the Act of 1487, though its jurisdiction, methods of trial and scale of punishments were quite different. It was, perhaps, not unnatural that this misunderstanding should have occurred, for apart from

179

meeting in the same room at Westminster it was commonly held that since penal legislation could be enforced only by special courts, unhampered by the common law traditions, Henry's tribunal must be the precursor of the later court.

Another offshoot of the Council's legal jurisdiction was the Court of Requests, which first appeared in 1483, and was probably modelled on an institution of the same name in France. It seemed unlikely to survive until Henry VII breathed new life into it. By origin, it was a court of 'poor men's causes' and of other civil suits relating to royal servants, which met under the Lord Privy Seal and the ecclesiastical lawyers on the Council. Its procedure was informal, its justice swift and cheap, compared with the older courts, and it soon attracted many litigants who were very far from being either poor or in the royal service. The King underlined the original intentions of the Court in 1495 by laying down that poor men should be exempt from fees and be assigned free legal aid.

Another development of these years was the re-appointment of a council to govern Wales and the Marches, which had been

The heraldic shields bear the labels: *The Marquesse of Dorsett Tho: Grey; The Earle of Northumberland Henry Algernons f Percy; The Earle of Surrey Thomas Howard Treasurer of England; The L...bury...*

The King processing to Parliament with his temporal and spiritual peers. This illustration was painted during the first years of Henry VIII's reign, but as the artist has represented the king as an old man it has been suggested that he based the scene upon one of Henry VII's processions. He is preceded by heralds and by Edward Stafford, Duke of Buckingham carrying the cap of state, and an unidentified peer bearing the sword of justice. The figures following the King include Thomas Grey, Marquess of Dorset, and Thomas Howard, Earl of Surrey.

established by Edward IV as a means of granting some degree of regional government to the Principality. Such a scheme was dear to Henry's heart. First his uncle, Jasper Tudor, was given wide powers for overseeing royal lands in Wales and enforcing law in an area which had caused trouble to the Crown throughout the Wars of the Roses; and then, as we have seen, Arthur, Prince of Wales was sent to Ludlow. The later Council in the North was foreshadowed in the appointment of the Earl of Surrey to oversee Yorkshire.

The High Court of Parliament, though an integral part of the constitution, met only when the King chose to summon it, to perform the essential tasks of voting taxes and passing the legislation that new policies required. There was still something of 'a national emergency' about the issue of writs for a new Parliament; the King needed monies for the French war or to have acts of attainder passed against rebels. There would have been little to commend the regular sitting of a body that sought to hold a 'grand inquest of the nation' as its price for providing revenue, and in fact most of the grievances aired by the men from the boroughs and shires concerned financial affairs. If Henry could manage to 'live of his own', meeting all the demands on his purse from the revenues from his estates, the ancient rights of the Crown and the proceeds of the customs, granted him for life in 1485, then he could dispense with Parliament. Taking prorogations into account, in his reign of twenty-four years there were only seven Parliaments, which sat for a total of sixty-six weeks. In the early years of the reign (1485–7 and 1489–91) Parliament met for an average of seven weeks a year, mostly in the late autumn or early spring; at that period there was much business necessary for settling the regime and giving it a sound financial base, yet after the dissolution of March 1491 the Houses did not re-assemble until the end of 1495. The sixth Parliament met for a few weeks only, in 1497, to discuss ways and means for the Scottish campaigns, but the seventh did not assemble until January 1504, when Henry received a rude rebuff from the Commons. Although his servant Edmund Dudley was Speaker, the House would not grant the £90,000 requested, but only £40,000 and the King deemed it politic to remit as much as a quarter of this sum and tap non-Parliamentary resources. It would not meet again in his reign. As Sir Thomas More noted, 'the gathering of money is the only thing that withdraweth the hearts of Englishmen from their Prince'.

Henry's Parliaments were not 'packed', as the outcry at the proposed levies in 1504 shows. Most of the legislation passed counted as 'government measures' and in some of the preambles to Acts, which were becoming useful vehicles for propaganda, one can detect the King's hand – as when in 1489 he declared that for him 'there is nothing more joyous than to know his subjects live peaceably under his laws'. Private members' bills were, however, more common and more likely to reach the statute book than in the later twentieth century. It was independent members who framed the first Navigation Act, 1489 (which required English merchants to use English ships for their exports), who reformed weights and measures in 1491 and who empowered Justices of the Peace to deal more effectively with riots in 1495.

The King's pragmatic approach to policy is well shown by his attitude to livery and maintenance. He could not at once curb the private retinues of great men, for if these were a potential source of civil disturbance they were also the nucleus of an army for his own service. In an age in which there was no standing army, it would have been absurd to have outlawed what amounted to a territorial reserve, and when Henry went to war he followed the customary practice of making 'indentures of war' with specific barons, who then enlisted their own companies. He always urged these great landowners to restrain the men in their livery from illegal conduct. The existing laws forbidding men below the rank of baron to retain men were executed with vigour and the King even found it necessary to forbid men from poaching on his own demesne by taking up tenants from the royal estates into their bands, exchanging the Tudor livery for their own. Time and again, statutes and royal proclamations reminded subjects of every degree of their duty of allegiance to the King which must take precedence over lesser loyalties to a tenant-in-chief. By 1502 Henry felt strong enough to forbid men in certain counties, including Kent and Sussex (who were not tenants of the Crown estate), to be retained by any man, since their service belonged to him alone, and when, two years later, Parliament met there was passed the renowned Statute against Liveries. Most of the Act repeated clauses of a measure of 1468, but the novelty was procedural. All cases of breach of the law were to be reported to the Court of King's Bench for trial in that Court or before the Council. Local justices had been unable to enforce prosecutions against great magnates who intimidated them and packed juries with their followers. By insisting on the removal of all cases to Westminster, the Act had teeth. Almost immediately Lord Abergavenny, a cousin of the King and a Councillor who had winked at the law, was brought to book. It was found that Abergavenny had been taking up no fewer than 471 retainers in Kent, a forbidden area, and he was fined the massive sum of £70,650. Another departure in the 1504 Act was a clause by which the King could license men to raise troops for the royal service. Henry could not do without the retinues of the great, but he had hedged about the arrangements with sufficient safeguards for guaranteeing his own ultimate control.

The new-style conciliar courts, some of which had precursors under the Yorkists, became termed by later lawyers 'the

Prerogative Courts', in contrast to the common law courts of Chancery, King's Bench and Common Pleas. They stemmed, indeed, from the royal prerogative – those inalienable rights under the law which Henry exercised by virtue of being an anointed king. After he had reigned for ten years, two serjeants-at-law, Robert Constable and Thomas Frowick, gave a series of lectures to benchers and students at the Inns of Court on the Royal Prerogative, showing in no sycophantic manner that Henry had been at pains to enforce to the full his feudal rights which his immediate predecessors had let slide. Under the feudal land system the magnates had held their estates as tenants-in-chief of the King by knight service, and from this much followed. As a recent commentator puts it, Henry's enlargement of his prerogative rights 'involved no abuses of the law' however burdensome the processes may have been; he had acted by 'a rigorous use of law and logic'.

During his first year he had appointed receivers-general in the different regions for dealing with lands he intended keeping in his own hands, and he at once tightened up the system of taking inquisitions on the deaths of tenants-in-chief and of all others suspected of holding property, however small, direct from the Crown, to discover the details and the identity and age of the heir. Too often minors had unlawfully succeeded to estates, when they should have been royal wards until they reached the age of twenty-one. The King instituted a series of far-reaching enquiries into concealments and evasions, to gain a great deal of essential information for the management of these properties, and kept the local officers in the shires, the escheators, on their toes. Strengthening the system of wardship and inheritance not only enabled the King to control his great land-owners, but also provided a most valuable source of revenue. Wardships, with the right to arrange the young person's marriage, were sold to the highest bidder. No heir to a tenancy-in-chief could take possession of his lands without 'suing for livery' and he could enter on his lands only by royal licence; fees were paid to the Crown at every stage. Paradoxically, the legal rights of livery and wardship were being extended for political and financial reasons at the very time at which feudal society, which had given them their purpose, had ceased to exist. By astute management, first by Reginald Bray

Master Bray

Item Receaved of Mast. by[t] bray by
thand of ... fayer of the ...
of ... knyght ... at the last ...

Master bray

Item Receaved of Mast. Bray by thand
of ... ... a praye for ...
of the knyght saladis Chapelevs & othe

Thabbot of Redyng

Item Receaved of thabbot of Redyng — ... li. iij s. iiij d.

Thoms Dakers

Item Receaved of thoms Dakers — ... li.

the lumbardes

Item Receaved of the lumbardes for
a licence for the byyng of ... li. s.

Sm ...

and John Heron, and then by Sir John Hussey, the King's annual revenue from wardships rose from £350 to over £6,000. In 1502 Hussey was appointed to a new office, Master of the Wards, which was the effective beginning of a new court, the Court of Wards and Liveries.

Other feudal rights which had long lain dormant were the customary dues enshrined in Magna Carta, which the King could demand of his subjects when his eldest son was knighted and his eldest daughter married. Henry levied both. A third feudal due, the payment of the King's ransom if he were captured by enemies, was not a matter Henry cared to think about!

Living 'of his own' for meeting day-to-day expenses of government entailed not only exploiting feudal rights but a rigorous control of Crown lands. Edward IV had managed these estates himself, using up-to-date business methods such as those favoured by great landowners, and instead of having the revenues paid into the Exchequer, which was notoriously slow and bureaucratic in its processes, he had these funds paid direct into his Chamber, the chief financial department of the royal household. After Bosworth, when the Yorkist Chamber system collapsed, the inexperienced Henry allowed rents and profits from his estates to go through the Exchequer, only to find that he received in a full year less than half the amount his predecessor had netted. He was extremely short of money and even claimed that he could not finance the feast of the Order of the Garter at Windsor. He soon realised that he must return to a system of Chamber finance, giving this the personal supervision which was essential. One after another, the accounts of the principal receivers were diverted from the Exchequer to the Chamber, where the documents were in a simple form, readily intelligible and (unlike Exchequer accounts) very legible. The process of audit was swift and the King himself annotated and signed the summaries of the Treasurer of the Chamber (see opposite). The pressure of paperwork forced Henry to develop a new signature – a flourish written without raising his pen from the paper, to save time. There was close supervision of the local receivers, surveyors and other officials by the key financiers at Court – Bray, Heron, and Sir Thomas Lovell.

A new procedure was devised to secure speedy payment of

OPPOSITE Book of receipts of Sir Thomas Lovell, Treasurer of the King's Chamber from 1489 to 1495. Each entry has been checked by Henry VII and is attested by his sign manual. The King altered his sign manual in August 1492, so he could write more quickly, to cope with the increase in paperwork, and the change can be seen by comparing the first two entries of the page.

BELOW Sir Thomas Lovell, Treasurer of the King's Chamber and one of the key financiers of the Court. He supervised Torrigiano's work on the tombs of Henry and his mother in Westminster Abbey, and the Florentine sculptor executed this bronze medallion which hangs by the monument to the Lady Margaret Beaufort.

money from Crown debtors. Men owing the King money were required to enter into bonds, with sureties, to pay their dues by a certain date. For sizeable debts they were also made to sign obligations undertaking to pay even larger sums than those technically due; this supplementary deed would automatically be cancelled by the prompt payment of the original sum. Large debts could be spread over several years – but at much higher rates. Defaulters were prosecuted in the courts, and at the end of the day this could mean confiscation of property and outlawry. The system worked extremely well from the King's point of view, for he knew months ahead the amount of money that should be coming into the Chamber and could plan his budget.

In his last years, he could do very well without the aid of Parliamentary grants for, besides the increased efficiency in exploiting his prerogative rights, the King took his cut from the increasing volume of foreign trade through customs duties. When his financial system was at its height, there was naturally a ground swell of discontent, and immediately upon his death his successor was forced to bow to popular pressure for the trial of the two men who had operated his fiscal machine, 'the ravening wolves' Empson and Dudley.

Both lawyers by training, they had become prominent members of the Council Learned in the Law, with Sir Richard Empson as Chancellor of the Duchy of Lancaster, President of that tribunal from 1505. A fresh examination of their activities suggests that these were no different in kind from the work performed earlier in the reign by Morton and Bray, and, like those good churchmen, the 'upstarts' worked within the law, for they were legal experts. Posterity has remembered Empson and Dudley with 'ignominy' simply because of their success. Like other royal servants living largely on fees, they took their pickings from clients who sought the King's favour through them, yet they knew better than to try to cheat Henry. They lived next door to each other near London Stone in Walbrook Ward in the City, and even this was counted against them. To achieve their tasks of calling in Henry's dues they employed informers, which wrankled with men brought up on the virtues of tax avoidance, evasions even. Dudley's account book shows that he achieved the incredible feat of netting £65,361 for the King in the financial year 1506–7. Of course, it became a talking-point that Thomas Kneysworth, Lord Mayor of London, and his two sheriffs were heavily fined for misdemeanours and that the Earl of Northumberland was ordered to pay £10,000 for abducting a royal ward, though most of this latter fine was to be remitted. It was the wealthy and high-ranking men who 'suffered most' as the chroniclers put it, for unlike the poor they had the means to pay. The backlash came with the demise of the Crown and a penitent Edmund Dudley, deprived of the protection of the master for whom he had worked so faithfully, could only admit that Henry VII had lost the hearts of his subjects by his insatiable greed for gold.

In these final years of the reign, several 'over-mighty' subjects were being controlled by suspended fines and made to enter recognisances for crippling sums to ensure their good behaviour. It was almost as if Henry VII 'governed by recognisance', one recent historian has remarked. Henry had cowed the baronage by remorseless manipulation of his fiscal rights. Men tied to his purse-strings bided their time and immediately on his son's accession persuaded him to act. Empson and Dudley were put in the Tower, great enquiries were set afoot into injustice and peculation, and even the new King's warrants which cancelled so many of the hated recognisances and bonds spoke of the activities of his financial agents 'against law, right and conscience to the evident overburdening and danger of our late father's soul'. The first Tudor, in re-establishing royal power and a strong administration, had pressed much too hard, and it is a matter of conjecture if, had he lived, he could have continued to maintain the pressure without risking overthrow. It would have been a vicious spiral, for Henry had set out to make himself solvent as the surest way of being able to keep his throne.

8 The Widower
1503-9

Arthur's death in 1502 almost broke Henry's heart, for from birth, as it were, the Prince had been groomed for the crown. Yet Henry still had a male heir in Prince Henry, now eleven, who seemed healthy enough, though it was another ten months before he was created Prince of Wales. Infant mortality remained the chief threat to the succession; in 1495 Henry had lost his third daughter, little Elizabeth, named after her mother, and five years later Prince Edmund had died. There was still a chance that he might father another prince as a further insurance, and a month after Arthur's burial Elizabeth of York began another pregnancy. This proved a severe test for the Queen's health and she was poorly all that summer. For her lying-in she had chosen the royal apartments on the upper floor of the White Tower of the Tower of London, next to the little Chapel of St John. Here in February 1503 she died, a week after giving birth to a baby girl, hastily christened Catherine, who did not survive her mother by many days.

Henry's cup of sorrow was indeed full, and to add to his cares he was about to lose his elder daughter, Margaret, nearly fourteen, who was to travel north to marry King James IV of Scotland. At the end of June Henry left London to escort her part of the way, staying for a day or so with his mother, and finally bade Margaret farewell at Collyweston in Northamptonshire. The wedding took place on 8 August at the Palace of Holyrood House, and was celebrated by Dunbar in his poem on *The Thistle and the Rose*, which prophesied in a mysterious way the union of the crowns of the two kingdoms, so long at enmity, which would come about exactly a hundred years later when James VI of Scotland went south to succeed Elizabeth I. Henry was never to see Margaret again, and the younger Henry and his sister Mary, just seven, would not meet her again for another thirteen years.

The Lady Margaret again became a widow with Derby's death in 1504. Now sixty-one, she had no further need of husbands and somewhat unnecessarily took a vow of chastity. But her son the King of England was only forty-six, and had no intention of remaining a widower if a suitable bride could be found. A day or so before leaving for the north with Princess Margaret, he had betrothed his sole surviving son to the widowed

ptit seruiteur qui no
ute vrape humilite v
auctie/ lequel par ma
pour eschieuir oyseul

Catherine of Aragon. Her father, Ferdinand of Spain, after a decent interval to allow for the appropriate show of grief at Arthur's death, had demanded that Henry should repay the first instalment of her marriage portion, amounting to 100,000 crowns, and that she should take effective possession of the dower lands assigned to her. King Henry did not intend giving way so easily and far from agreeing to refund the sum already paid him, he demanded of right to be recompensed for the residue of Catherine's marriage portion. At any rate he had no intention of allowing the girl to return to Spain, for she was too valuable a pawn in the diplomatic game. For the moment, then, it was politic to allow the young Duke of York to take on an obligation to marry his brother's widow, but in the arrangements made there was plenty of room for manœuvre.

Then King Henry suddenly announced that he would marry his daughter-in-law himself. Of course a papal dispensation would be necessary, but Catherine would as a result become Queen Consort of England overnight, instead of having to wait for Henry's death, if she were to marry the Prince of Wales. The girl's mother, Isabella, was a realist; not very far from death herself, she doubted (and events confirmed her intuition) whether Catherine would have much longer as Henry's wife than she had enjoyed as Arthur's and she feared that the King could not give her a child. On this reckoning, Catherine would spend most of her days as a Queen-Dowager, without influence and with little money, so that Prince Henry would be a far safer bet and a more suitable husband, too, on grounds of age. Isabella had no hesitation in telling Henry to look elsewhere for a wife; his proposal 'would be an evil thing, the mere mention of which offends the ears, and we would not for anything in the world that it should take place'. Henry must undertake to honour the contract between his son and his daughter-in-law. Nevertheless Queen Isabella realised that the Anglo-Spanish alliance needed strengthening and that if Henry Tudor married into another royal House there could be ruinous consequences for Spain. Thus, on reflection, she recommended most fervently the charms of the widowed Queen of Naples, then resident in Spain, who was the daughter of Ferdinand's sister; she was no more than twenty-six, amiable, rich and 'particularly well-qualified to console him in his deep affliction'.

Marguerite d'angleterre D'ugne lesture fens de Henry vij.^e
D'vij d'angleterre femme de Jaques iiij Roy d'escosse

Margaret Tudor,
Henry VII's elder daughter,
who married James IV,
King of Scots, in 1503.
Drawing from *Recueil
d'Arras*.

Henry found the suggestion of the Queen of Naples intrigu-
ing, and sent ambassadors to make full enquiries about the lady,
her appearance and personality, her health and the state of her
finances. Three discreet envoys, Francis Marsin, James Bray-
brooke and John Stile, patiently went through Henry's ques-
tionnaire and set down their diplomatic answers as honestly as
they could. They failed to 'come to any perfect knowledge of
her stature, by reason of her wearing slippers, after the manner
of the country. A man could not lightly perceive the features
of her body, for that she wore a great mantle of cloth.' What
about her complexion and her use of cosmetics? 'The Queen',
they answered, 'is not painted; of a good compass, amiable
round and fat; cheerful, not frowning; a demure, shame-faced
countenance; a person of few words, but spoken with a
womanly laughing cheer and good humour.' Her skin was fair,

IACOBVS · 4 · D · GRATIA
REX · SCOTORVM

LEFT James IV, King of Scots, who married Margaret Tudor, Henry's elder daughter, in 1503.

BELOW Louis XII, King of France, who married Mary Tudor, Henry's younger daughter, in 1513. He is depicted on this Limoges enamel triptych with his second wife, Anne of Brittany, whom he had married in 1499 (after divorcing his first consort, Joanna) to keep the duchy of of Brittany for the Crown.

her hair probably brown. Henry clearly became most interested in this vivacious widow as he read further in the despatch that her lips were round and full, her neck comely, and her breasts 'great and full and trussed somewhat high'. The King had asked the envoys to find out whether her breath was sweet, yet they 'could never come near to her feasting, but at other times have approached her visage as nigh as they conveniently could but never felt any savour of spices, and believe her to be a sweet savour'. They gathered from her physician that her health was remarkably good and mentioned that she enjoyed her food, though drank moderately, preferring water to wine. Henry had asked them to commission an artist to paint a skilful likeness of the Queen, but they were unable to find a suitable man. The sting was in the tail, because at the very end of their paper they stated that her jointure was non-existent, for she lived solely on a meagre allowance from Ferdinand I. She had no reversion to the crown of Naples and it was obvious that despite her many attractive qualities she was both poor and politically impotent.

Soon after Henry received this frank report Isabella of Castile died. While Henry remained a widower, Ferdinand of Aragon – not content with the consolations of a series of mistresses – hastily married a Princess of Navarre. Henry turned in disgust from the royal House of Spain and required the Prince of Wales to register a formal protest against his betrothal to Catherine and the inadequacy of the papal dispensation. As an alternative to Spanish marriages, Henry opened negotiations for a full family compact with the House of Habsburg, itself already connected with Spain through the marriage of Joanna of Castile to the Archduke Philip of Burgundy, eldest son of the Holy Roman Emperor. With Isabella's death, Joanna now succeeded her as Queen of Castile, though for the moment she stayed in the Netherlands. Henry himself rather fancied Philip's sister, the Archduchess Margaret of Austria, and in January 1506 a marriage with her seemed a distinct possibility. Fate seemed to play into his hands when Philip the Handsome, now titular King of Castile and his Queen Joanna, bound from the Netherlands for Spain, were driven by a gale on to the shore near Weymouth, Dorset. Joanna stayed for a few days to recuperate at Wolverton Manor, for she had been badly shaken by

her experiences, and subsequently presented the house with some fine mahogany panelling; her husband rode on to Winchester, where Prince Henry welcomed him, and to Catherine of Aragon's delight her sister and brother-in-law were soon being royally entertained at Windsor. Catherine asked Philip to show the company one of the intricate Spanish dances after dinner, but he coyly refused: 'I am a mariner', he said, joking at the recent shipwreck, 'and yet you would make me dance.' Princess Mary, aged ten, gladly showed her skill in playing the lute and the regals. 'She played very well', it was noted, and 'in every way she behaved herself very well'. There was feasting and merriment for a month, during which Philip was installed as a Knight of the Garter, and after this ceremony the two Kings signed a strict treaty of alliance, offensive as well as defensive, with each solemnly undertaking to be 'a friend of the friends and an enemy of the enemies' of the other. Philip signed, he said, not merely for himself, but for his father, the Emperor Maximilian. At the banquet which followed, King Henry said 'You have seen the round table at Winchester, of which so much has been said and written; but I hope that in future men will talk of *this* table at which a true, perpetual friendship was made between the Empire of Rome, the Kingdom of Castile, Flanders and Brabant, and the Kingdom of England.'

Henry had Philip in his power and was in a position to dictate the terms of the supplementary agreements. His visitor undertook to surrender the exiled Earl of Suffolk, who was to be promised a full pardon for past offences. Within the month the 'White Rose of England' was duly brought to Calais and thence to the Tower, where he remained a close prisoner so long as Henry lived. Suffolk was to be executed in 1513, his proximity to the crown and his past intrigues never forgiven. There was also a commercial agreement which placed English traders in the Netherlands in most favourable circumstances, for they were to be exempt from many local tolls in Antwerp and elsewhere, while Philip's subjects were to pay in England the dues fixed by the treaty of 1496, but never fully imposed. A treaty on such terms, branded by the Flemings as the *Intercursus Malus*, would have strained the Anglo-Burgundian alliance to breaking-point had it ever been ratified, and in December 1507 the most serious grievances in the concessions extracted from Philip were

OPPOSITE Margaret of Austria, the eldest daughter of the Emperor Maximilian I and Mary of Burgundy. She had been married to Juan, the only son and heir of Ferdinand and Isabella, but he died within a few months of marriage. In 1503, Henry VII decided that Margaret would be an ideal consort for him, but the lady was not over-eager for the match. Portrait by Maître de Moulin.

LEFT Charles of Ghent, Maximilian's eldest grandson and heir to the vast empires of the Habsburgs and the Catholic Majesties of Spain. In 1507, Henry VII and Maximilian signed a treaty whereby the seven-year-old Charles was to marry Mary Tudor, Henry's younger daughter. Although a solemn betrothal ceremony took place, Mary and Charles were never to marry.

RIGHT Mary Tudor, who was celebrated for her beauty and grace. Despite her betrothal to Charles she was eventually married to Louis XII of France – a short-lived liaison.

alleviated. Finally, in return for Henry's undertaking to safe-guard the Netherlands during his absence in Spain, Philip promised him the hand of his sister Margaret of Austria, who would bring with her a goodly marriage portion of three hundred thousand crowns and an annual income of a tenth of that sum. This union of Habsburg and Tudor was to be buttressed by two further marriages – of Princess Mary with Philip's son Charles of Ghent, and of Henry, Prince of Wales with his daughter Eleanora. Both Kings were united in their desire to outwit Ferdinand of Aragon.

The marriage treaty between Henry VII and Margaret of Austria was ratified on 15 May, and under its terms the children of the marriage would succeed to any sovereignty in Spain, Flanders or elsewhere to which their mother had a right. As it happened, neither party was anxious to proceed to a betrothal. Once Philip the Handsome had reached Spain, he met the Cortes of Castile at Valladolid to force his father-in-law Ferdinand to give way to all his demands for ruling the separate kingdom of Castile. This triumph was short-lived, for on 25 September 1506 Philip died at Burgos in his twenty-ninth year, and Ferdinand was quick to regain control of Castile as guardian of his widowed daughter Joanna. As soon as Henry heard of Philip's death he made urgent enquiries about the hand of his widow, already being called 'the mad Joanna'. He had been impressed by her fragile beauty when she had been his surprise guest at Windsor and he needed a lot of convincing that she was as feather-brained, let alone as deranged, as her father made out. The Spanish ambassador in London told his master that the English 'seem little to mind her insanity, especially as they have been told that it would not prevent her from bearing children'. Certainly the ambassador reckoned that Henry would make an ideal husband and if she married him she would 'soon recover her reason'. Alas, Joanna's behaviour confirmed everyone's worst suspicions. She refused to have her husband buried, but set out on a second honeymoon, dressed as a bride, into the mountains of Granada, raving incantations over Philip's coffin. Soon she had to be confined for her own safety and stayed under close surveillance until her death in 1555.

The Emperor Maximilian had revived the question of Princess Mary's marriage to his grandson Charles of Ghent, which had first been mooted in 1499. At last, in December 1507, a fresh treaty was signed, by which the boy Archduke, now almost seven, undertook to marry Mary, a petite, graceful girl three years his senior, before the following Easter, by proxy or in person, with a view to the celebration of their nuptials when the bridegroom reached his fourteenth birthday. With his father's death, Charles was the heir-presumptive of the entire Habsburg and Spanish dominions in Europe and the New World, and was easily the greatest match for any Princess. For the first time, Henry could feel himself on equal footing with the Holy Roman Emperor. Henry was to pay a sizeable dowry for Mary and the promise of it at once eased Maximilian's problems with the banking houses at Augsburg and elsewhere, while the signing of the treaty made for immediate improvements in the commercial relations between 'the old Burgundian inheritance' and England, which was the cornerstone of Tudor prosperity.

Ferdinand of Aragon, still incensed with Henry over the matter of Catherine's dowry, contrived to have Princess Mary's proxy marriage postponed, if not abandoned, but eventually in December 1508 a substitute bridegroom in the person of the Sieur de Bergues arrived with a splendid retinue of Flemings and Spaniards, bearing the Emperor's wedding gift, a diamond *fleur-de-lys* of dazzling beauty, for which Henry was later to receive a bill for 50,000 crowns. The ceremony took place in the Queen's Presence Chamber at Richmond, which had been scarcely used since the death of Elizabeth of York. Here, after speeches from Archbishop Warham, the President of Flanders and others, de Bergues approached the dais beneath the canopy of State, where Mary sat alone on a low stool, and extolled the Archduke Charles's utter devotion to her. Mary replied haltingly, almost overcome with emotion, so that she needed prompting to repeat the speech in which her father knew she was word perfect. Holding the proxy bridegroom's hand she accepted 'the Lord Charles' and vowed to hold him as her true husband for the rest of her life. Then de Bergues kissed her on the lips and placed on the fourth finger of her right hand the wedding ring. A formal contract was signed and after Mass, at which the men and the ladies sat separately, there was a splendid banquet. Mary and Catherine of Aragon dined apart, but were allowed to watch the tournament from a safe gallery. The eight-year-old Charles had sent Mary a diamond set in pearls and enscribed with the words from the Vulgate, 'Mary hath chosen the better part, which shall not be taken from her', and a charming letter asking after her health, signed *'votre bon mari'*. In this age of matrimonial diplomacy the most confidently executed betrothals could be overturned by the exigencies of politics and Mary Tudor was never to marry Charles. Within six years she would be forced by her brother to take on that old *roué*, Louis XII of France.

Henry, Duke of York, Henry VII's second son and his eventual successor as Henry VIII. He led a sheltered life as a child, and was destined by his father for a career in the Church.

Ferdinand's eyes were on Venice, not on Richmond, and in the month of the proxy marriage he became a party to the League of Cambrai, formed between Margaret of Austria as Regent of the Netherlands, and the Cardinal of Rouen for a joint attack under papal blessing to despoil the Republic of Venice. If Henry VII felt that Ferdinand had outwitted him, he at least rejoiced in keeping clear of expensive Continental commitments.

Remaining a widower, Henry became increasingly isolated. He rarely saw his mother and he refused to see Catherine of

Aragon, who endured almost the life of a prisoner in Durham
House in the Strand, living frugally with her argumentative
servants. Prince Henry, who had been affianced to her and then
required to register a protest about having to contract the
marriage, lacked the independence which his brother Arthur
had enjoyed well before his own brief marriage with
Catherine. Instead of being assigned a separate household as
Prince of Wales and sent to Ludlow Castle, young Henry was
kept under close surveillance at his father's Court and treated
very much as a child; some ambassadors even thought he was
being brought up more like a princess than as male heir to the
throne. His apartments could be reached only through the
King's and he took his exercise in the palace grounds well supervised. Youths of his own age, however, shared his schooling –
such as Charles Brandon and Edward Neville, with whom he
played tennis, rode and tested his skill in the butts. At his books,
no less than in athletics and musical accomplishments, the
Prince showed remarkable proficiency, yet his father refused
to spoil him. Jealous of his own power and reluctant to think
that his reign was shortening, King Henry gave the boy no
instruction in the art of government and apparently never considered allowing him to be present when he gave audiences to
envoys or ecclesiastics or when he sat with his Councillors. In
consequence Henry VIII came to the crown without any
serious preparation for wearing it.

Henry's health was declining and, no less worrying, his sight
was deteriorating, though few besides his mother were aware
of his terrible fear of going blind. In vain he bathed his eyes with
traditional lotions 'to make bright the sight', concocted from
fennell water, roses and celandine – but to no purpose. The King
who himself had patiently checked accounts and read des-
patches, feared being cheated at home and outwitted abroad
if he could not retain a firm grasp on paperwork. Certainly from
his forties, he gave the impression of a man worn out by the
care of office; but sovereigns dared not contemplate retirement
in so uncertain a world and the future Emperor Charles V – the
Charles of Ghent whom Princess Mary never married – created
a precedent when fifty years on he voluntarily abdicated and
withdrew to a monastery. The King described by the chronicler
Polydore Vergil in his final years does not appear as a man in

Anno ħ o 5 29 octobᵹ ꞯꞯꞯago ħꞧꞯ₂ich vii ᵗᵃꞧⁱᵗᵘᵍᵧ ᵗᵍᵗᵉ illuſtꞯſſⁱꞯ
oꞧꞯꞯata ꝑ ħꞯ₂ꞯaꞯꞯ zꞯꞯꞯₖ ꝟₒ ᵗᵍₑₗₑ   ꞯꞯꞯꞯaꞯꞯꞯꞯ

serious decline: 'His body was slender but well-built and strong; his height above average. His appearance was remarkably attractive and his face was cheerful, especially when speaking; his eyes were small and blue, his teeth few, poor and blackish; his hair was thin and grey; his complexion pale.'

In these latter days Henry often felt poorly with the coming of spring. In 1509 he was not well enough to follow his customary observance of Holy Week, reciting the psalms as the priests stripped to the boards the rich trappings of the chapel at Richmond Palace on Maundy Thursday, or creeping to the Cross on Good Friday, though he made a special effort to attend divine service on Easter Day. Within a fortnight he was dead, prematurely worn out by the responsibilities of kingship at the age of fifty-two. It was fittingly at Richmond, the palace he had himself built out of the ruins of Sheen, that he died on 21 April 1509, after calling his son to his bedside to extract from him a promise, so it is said, to marry Catherine of Aragon, the spurned Princess. Henry hoped that those responsible for his funeral arrangements would follow to the letter his precise instructions, 'to avoid always damnable pomp and other outrageous superfluities'. On earth kings were different in kind, as well as degree, from their subjects, but once under the shadow of death they, too, must trust in God's infinite mercy.

Never popular with his subjects, as the open-handed Edward IV had been, suspicious to the end of men's loyalty (for he had been utterly disillusioned by the treachery of friends he had trusted), he had become a recluse since the death of Elizabeth of York. Henry's passing did not evoke a spontaneous display of heartfelt national mourning, as would mark his granddaughter Elizabeth's death. All eyes were on his successor, the young, athletic Prince who would assuredly usher in a new age. The final years of the old reign had, indeed, been a period of reaction during which the financial resources of the Crown were exploited to the hilt. With Henry VII a widower, despite his efforts to re-marry, the Court of these years lacked the grace and dignity which only the presence of a queen could ensure. Richmond Palace had become rather gloomy, the atmosphere celibate and monastic. Bishop Fisher's funeral sermon suggested, not without justification, that Henry VII had latterly

OPPOSITE Henry VII's Chapel in Westminster Abbey, which is dominated by the elaborate and magnificent fan vault. In the lower part of the illustration stands the bronze grille which surrounds the tombs of Henry and Elizabeth of York.

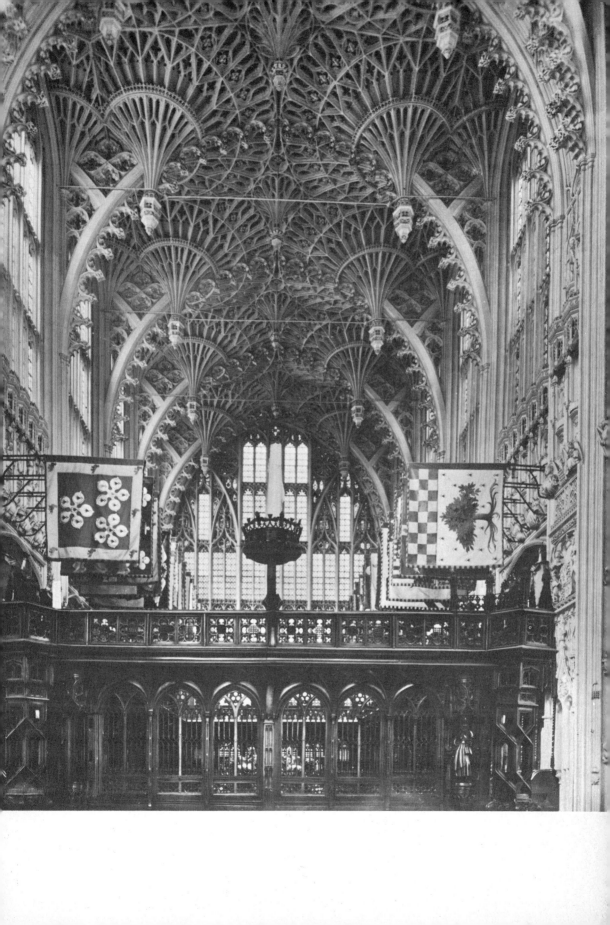

been more of a pilgrim seeking a crown of glory in the next world than a ruler who was a past master of diplomatic practice.

Henry had begun building the chapel at Westminster Abbey that was to be his finest memorial, not for himself, but as a shrine for the murdered King Henry VI. But, when there were obstacles from the Papacy to the Lancastrian King's canonisation, his bones remained at Windsor and the new chapel became transformed as Henry VII's own last resting-place. The key events of his reign, his coronation and marriage, had taken place in the Abbey, and here he was buried. The foundation stone of the chapel had been laid in January 1503, a month before his wife's death, and eighteen months later Henry caused an elaborate series of foundation indentures to be drawn up between himself, the Abbot and Chapter and the heads of various other religious houses for the future celebration of services and distribution of alms in his chapel; one such indenture showing the seals of the parties protected by silver cases, enamelled with shields of arms, is illustrated on page 210. The King had also prepared for the chapel a volume of ordinances which was beautifully illuminated with the royal arms supported by a Welsh dragon and a greyhound, his badge of the red rose and his mother's device of a portcullis. These ordinances, supplemented by the King's Will, would inaugurate an unceasing round of prayer for the repose of his soul after death, praise to the Almighty and almsgiving at his tomb. A separate college of priests was established to serve the chapel. The relics displayed there for veneration included a piece of the True Cross, set in gold and jewelled, and one of the legs of St George. The silk and velvet vestments, made in Florence, were embroidered with Tudor badges and devices. The chapel itself, which owed something to Sir Reginald Bray's sketch design, was not to be completed until 1519 by the King's mason, Robert Vertue, and even then the royal tombs remained unfinished. Henry had charged his executors with the task of commissioning a great Renaissance sculptor to undertake this work and as a result Pietro Torrigiano, who had been working under Borgia patronage in Rome, came to England in 1512 to execute the tombs, with their life-like effigies of Henry Tudor, his wife and his mother, and a marble altar.

Henry's will was a testament of late medieval beliefs. He had

OPPOSITE The illustration of September in the *Golf Book*, which contains leaves of miniatures and borders taken from *The Hours of the Blessed Virgin*, painted by Flemish artists at about 1500. Below the ploughing, sowing and harrowing are children playing with marbles and stilts.

Henry VII's Tomb in Westminster Abbey

In his will Henry VII left detailed instructions on the erection of a monument to himself and his Queen, Elizabeth of York, to stand in the middle of his Chapel at Westminster. The King's executors, acting on his instructions, invited Pietro Torrigiano to come to England. Torrigiano was a Florentine sculptor who had studied under Ghirlandaio and, according to Vasari, quarrelled so fiercely with Michelangelo that he broke his nose. For Henry he created the first and finest Renaissance monuments in England.

BELOW Henry and Elizabeth, wrought in gilt bronze, lying side by side on the black marble tomb, with cherubs seated at each corner. The tomb, completed by 1518, is surrounded by a bronze screen or enclosure, produced by a Flemish craftsman referred to as Thomas Ducheman in the Chapel accounts. He has decorated the gilt with little figures of the red dragon of Wales and the greyhound of Richmond.

ABOVE The red dragon of Wales, the beast
chosen by Henry Tudor as his personal
symbol when he planned his invasion of
England in 1485 and his attack upon the
white boar of Richard III. This stone example
stands overlooking Henry's tomb.

prayed from childhood, he said, to his Saviour who had created him out of nothing, and constantly had asked for His mercy. He confessed his sins and his personal unworthiness in the full knowledge that he could attain life everlasting only through the merits of Christ's passion and of God's infinite grace. He called on the Blessed Virgin Mary, the saints, angels and heavenly host and the blessed company of the faithful to pray for him in his hour of need. He then turned to his benefactions in which religion and finance, the abiding interests of his later years, were entwined. Henry ordained that a month after his death ten thousand Masses were to be said for his soul in all the churches of greater London, for which each priest responsible would be paid 6d a service – considerably more than the average rate of payment. A score of the greatest religious foundations in the land were to keep his *obit*, the anniversary of his death, in perpetuity. There were separate bequests to the Carthusians of London and Sheen, near Richmond Palace, and since the friars of Greenwich could, through their vows of poverty, acquire nothing he made arrangements for their orchard wall to be rebuilt of brick. Henry set aside £2,000 for relieving the sick and needy, half the sum to be distributed at his tomb, the rest taken by visitors to the bedridden. To King's College, Cambridge he left £5,000 out of reverence to Henry VI, and there were funds for improving the main roads between Windsor, Westminster, Richmond and Canterbury, to make them pilgrims' ways. He asked that silver statues of himself, shown in the act of praying, be set up at the shrines of St Edward the Confessor, St Thomas of Canterbury and Our Lady of Walsingham in Norfolk. Finally, every church in the realm that had not a pyx or little box for the reserved sacrament of the altar, was to be provided with one of silver, decorated with the royal arms, the rose and the portcullis. Pious to the end, Henry saw himself in the line of English kings who had been great benefactors of the Church, from the Confessor through Henry III and Henry VI. But the medieval world which venerated the relics of holy men at their shrines would pass all too soon. Westminster Abbey escaped the excesses of the extreme Protestants in Edward VI's reign, yet in a fury of iconoclasm Roundhead soldiers would shatter the coloured glass and chip away at Torrigiano's marble altar, with its terracotta angels,

In 1513, Pietro Torrigiano also began work on the tomb of Lady Margaret Beaufort, Henry's mother who died in 1509, a few weeks after her son. Torrigiano has depicted her in widow's dress, with a hood and long mantle, and with her wrinkled hands raised in prayer. On her pillow are embossed her symbols – the Tudor rose and the Beaufort portcullis.

during the Civil War. The relics have vanished and the splendid ornaments have gone, but the tomb of the founder of the Tudor dynasty survives unharmed and the wonderful fabric of the chapel, the finest expression of late Gothic architecture, stands seemingly indestructible.

When Shakespeare, nearly ninety years later, began to write his cycle of plays on English history, from Richard II to Henry VIII, he never attempted to portray the years between Bosworth and Wolsey's rule. Though, understandably, the dramatist had not chosen to tackle the drama of Henry VIII's reign while his daughter still reigned, he still left Henry Tudor as the victor on Bosworth Field in the moment of his triumph, heralding a new

dawn, and he never thought it worthwhile to delineate his character as it developed under the stress of events when he was king. The reason is not far to seek. Once Henry had trounced the Yorkist opposition at the Battle of Stoke there was little of real drama to come. Dealing with Perkin Warbeck and the Cornish rebels seemed in retrospect a tame affair compared with the touch-and-go campaign of 1485. Henry had given England internal peace and prosperity and a reputation in Europe. He had so successfully established the rule of his House that Henry VIII came to the throne unchallenged and on the crest of a wave of popularity, simply because he was in age, character and outlook so very different from his father. Henry VII had become master in his own house and solvent – characteristics of a successful businessman rather than of a Caesar – and the idealism he had exemplified in his stand against Richard III had become suffused in a personal quest for spiritual peace. On such solid foundations were the glories of sixteenth-century England built.

OPPOSITE The portrait effigy of Henry VII from his tomb. Torrigiano worked from a wooden funeral effigy of the King, made from his death mask, and still kept in the Abbey.

The Tudor claim to the Crown

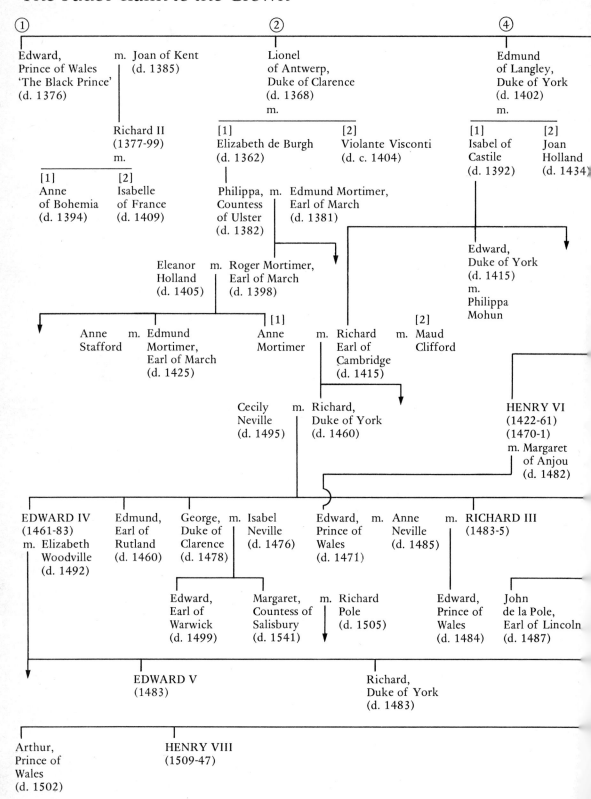

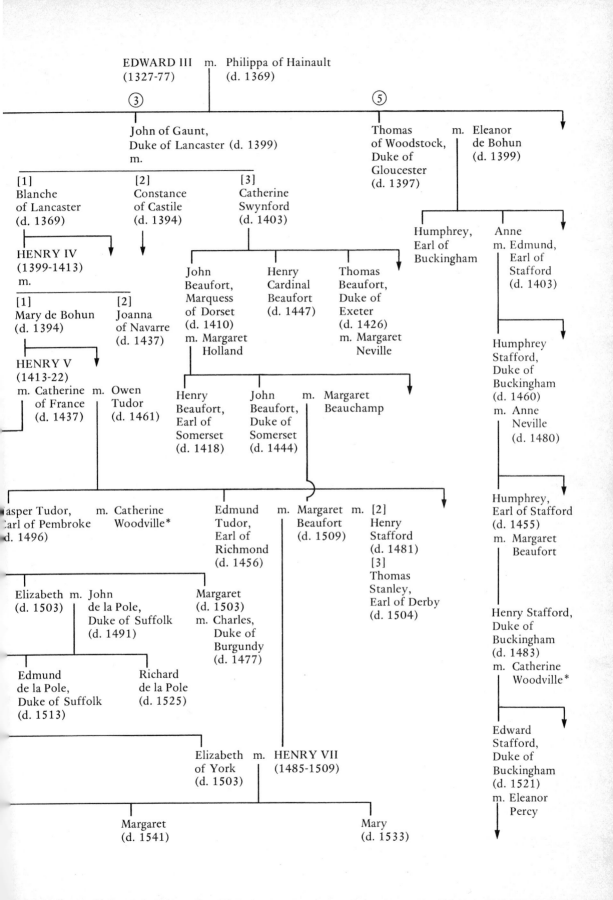

EDWARD III   m.   Philippa of Hainault
(1327-77)   (d. 1369)
    ③   ⑤

John of Gaunt,   Thomas   m. Eleanor
Duke of Lancaster (d. 1399)   of Woodstock,   de Bohun
m.   Duke of   (d. 1399)
                                         Gloucester
[1]   [2]   [3]   (d. 1397)
Blanche   Constance   Catherine
of Lancaster   of Castile   Swynford
(d. 1369)   (d. 1394)   (d. 1403)
                                         Humphrey,   Anne
                                         Earl of   m. Edmund,
HENRY IV   Buckingham   Earl of
(1399-1413)   Stafford
m.   John   Henry   Thomas   (d. 1403)
                 Beaufort, Cardinal   Beaufort,
[1]   [2]   Marquess   Beaufort   Duke of
Mary de   Joanna of Dorset (d. 1447) Exeter
Bohun   of Navarre (d. 1410)   (d. 1426)   Humphrey
(d. 1394) (d. 1437) m. Margaret   m. Margaret   Stafford,
                        Holland   Neville   Duke of
HENRY V   Buckingham
(1413-22)   (d. 1460)
m. Catherine m. Owen   Henry   John   m. Margaret   m. Anne
   of France   Tudor   Beaufort,   Beaufort, Beauchamp   Neville
   (d. 1437)   (d. 1461) Earl of   Duke of   (d. 1480)
                        Somerset   Somerset
                        (d. 1418)   (d. 1444)
                                                          Humphrey,
                                                          Earl of Stafford
Jasper Tudor,   m. Catherine   Edmund   m. Margaret m. [2]   (d. 1455)
Earl of Pembroke   Woodville* Tudor,   Beaufort   Henry m. Margaret
(d. 1496)   Earl of   (d. 1509)   Stafford Beaufort
                               Richmond   (d. 1481)
                               (d. 1456)   [3]
                                                        Thomas
Elizabeth m. John   Margaret   Stanley,
(d. 1503)   de la Pole,   (d. 1503)   Earl of Derby
             Duke of Suffolk   m. Charles,   (d. 1504)
             (d. 1491)   Duke of
                                 Burgundy   Henry Stafford,
                                 (d. 1477)   Duke of
Edmund   Richard   Buckingham
de la Pole,   de la Pole   (d. 1483)
Duke of Suffolk (d. 1525)   m. Catherine
(d. 1513)   Woodville*

                    Elizabeth m. HENRY VII
                    of York   (1485-1509)
                    (d. 1503)   Edward
                                                       Stafford,
                                                       Duke of
                                                       Buckingham
         Margaret   Mary   (d. 1521)
         (d. 1541)   (d. 1533)   m. Eleanor
                                                          Percy

Select bibliography

THE KING

The most detailed, and the most recent biography of Henry VII is by
S. B. Chrimes (1972). R. L. Storey's *The Reign of Henry* VII (1968)
discusses with great clarity the King and the problems facing England
before and after his accession. Lord Bacon's *The Life of Henry* VII
(1622) is superb prose but shaky history, for it was written out of
deference to James I, the first of the Stuarts, who expected to see
himself portrayed in this account of the first of the Tudors – another
'Solomon of England' and 'arbiter of Europe'. Many subsequent
writers were misled by Bacon's interpretation of Henry's achieve-
ments, but a readable study in that old-fashioned mould is James
Gairdner's *Henry the Seventh* (1889).

THE REIGN

Accounts of the reign will be found in J. D. Mackie, *The Earlier Tudors,
1485–1558* (Oxford History of England vol. 7, 1957); G. R. Elton,
England Under the Tudors (1956) and H. A. L. Fisher, *Political History
of England, 1485–1547* (1913 edn.). *The Reign of Henry* VII *from Contemporary Sources* (ed. A. F. Pollard, 3 vols., 1913–14) is an invaluable
quarry. Denys Hay's edition, with translation, of *The Anglica
Historia of Polydore Vergil, 1485–1537* has been published by the Royal
Historical Society (1950). K. W. H. Pickthorn, *Early Tudor Government: Henry* VII (1949) is an illuminating study of domestic policy,
while the relevant chapters of R. B. Wernham's *Before the Armada*
(1966) discuss foreign affairs.

SOCIETY

J. R. Lander, *Conflict and Stability in 15th-Century England* (1969) is full
of insight. H. Maynard Smith, *Pre-Reformation England* (1938)
contains a most readable account of church life – and much else – in
town and country. David Knowles, *The Religious Orders in England*
vols. 2 and 3 (1955, 1959) and A. Hamilton Thompson, *The English
Clergy and their Organization in the Later Middle Ages* (1947) are detailed,
stimulating surveys. *A Relation of the Island of England*, written *c.* 1500
by an Italian has been edited and translated for the Camden Society by
C. A. Sneyd (1847).

ECONOMIC AFFAIRS

Among a spate of recent monographs the most relevant are – E. M.
Carus-Wilson, *Medieval Merchant Venturers* (1954); A. R. Bridbury,
Economic Growth: England in the Later Middle Ages (1962); and J. A.
Williamson, *The Cabot Voyages and Bristol Discovery Under Henry* VII
(Hakluyt Society, 1962).

EDUCATION AND THE ARTS

Joan Simon, *Education and Society in Tudor England* (1966); H. S.
Bennett, *English Books and Readers, 1475–1557* (1952); J. H. Harvey,
Gothic England (1947); G. Webb, *Architecture in Britain in the Later
Middle Ages* (1956); and E. D. Mackerness, *A Social History of English
Music* (1966).

Index